Tennis
Inside the Zone

32 Mental Training Workouts for Champions

What if <u>one thing</u> could change EVERYTHING...?

game. changer

By Rob Polishook, M.A., C.P.C.

Tennis on the Brain!

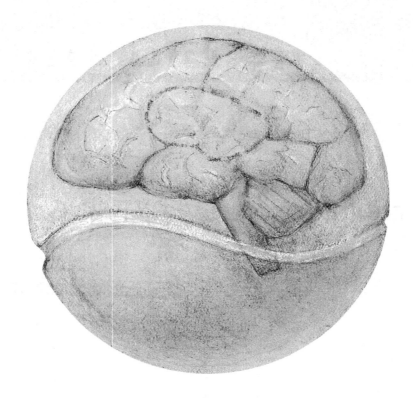

Copyright © 2013 Inside the Zone Sports Performance Group, LLC

Brain Ball design by Liz Buckley
Cover Design by Kellie Patterson

TENNIS INSIDE THE ZONE:
32 Mental Training Workouts for Champions

ISBN : 978-0-9891862-1-6

rob@insidethezone.com

How to Use This Book

Tennis Inside the Zone: Mental Training Workouts for Champions can be read and experienced in different ways. Initially, I suggest browsing through the table of contents to gain a broad overview. You will notice there are four sections, similar to how a match would unfold: Off-Court, Pre-Match, Match, and Post-Match. Then browse the individual workouts; each one also has four parts. These include:

- Quotes from the pros

- Principles which serve as a foundation

- A mental training article

- Interactive worksheet which ties the quotes, principles and article together.

These four parts (quotes, principles, article and worksheet) create what I have coined a "Mental Training Workout." The goal of the workout is to experientially guide you through the mental training concept. I hope they help you to confidently and purposefully incorporate the mental side of tennis into your game plan.

Now that you're familiar with the book's layout, I suggest you read the book in one of the following ways:

Start with a random section or specific workout that resonates with you. For example, maybe you're having trouble closing out a match? Go to the workout "OMG... I'm Nervous! What Do I Do? — Five Ways to Work Through Pre-Match Jitters." After reading the quotes, principles and article, take some time to think about them, and ask yourself a few questions: What does this workout mean to me? How might it apply to my situation? How could I incorporate the principles into my game? If I did, what might happen? How and when will I do it? Lastly, pick up your pen and complete the mental training workout. Take your time and approach each workout with P.I.P. (purpose, intention, and passion). Each workout might take between 15 and 45 minutes to complete.

Tennis Inside the Zone can be experienced by simply reading and completing the workouts from the front of the book to the back of the book, highlighting the parts which resonate with you.

Choose a partner and work through the workouts together. This is a great opportunity to share ideas.

Coaches, teachers, parents and sport psychology professionals can facilitate the workouts in a group or team setting, encouraging the players to share their experiences. Maybe picking out the key points and how the player could implement the teaching.

Contents

What Are Mental Training Workouts?

Tennis Inside the Zone: Mental Training Workouts for Champions allows you, the player, coach or parent, to seamlessly integrate the mental game with the tactical, strategic and physical game of tennis. Dedicating this time and discipline will improve your overall game. Over the years, I have observed players making time for on-court drills, practice, matches, and off-court fitness focusing on flexibility, strength and conditioning. This same commitment and intention must be made for the mental game. It's the "glue" that holds everything together.

Tennis Inside the Zone consists of 32 cutting-edge mental training "*workouts.*" Each *workout* highlights a specific mental training principle, such as focusing on what you can control, how to use imagery in match preparation, creating rituals for yourself, or managing negative self-talk. Specifically, each *workout* includes quotes from the pros, key principles, an in-depth article, and an experiential interactive *workout* for the player to complete.

Improving a player's mental game in tennis or any sport takes time. It's a process, during which the athlete will undoubtedly experience moments of feeling in control, moments of frustration, and moments where progress simply is not evident. In fact, it is much like improving the technical, physical, or strategic aspects of one's game. Each step builds on the previous one, like a growing tree: first come the seeds, then the roots, then the trunk, then the branches, then the leaves, and finally the fruits!

The discipline to allocate real time to complete a *workout* for the mental game demonstrates dedication, understanding, and purpose. Oftentimes, when a player works on the mental game it happens only after match play, drills, fitness, schoolwork, and video games are completed! In many cases, players, parents or coaches don't even think about the impact of the mental game until a bad loss or upset happens. I know, because this is when most of my clients come to seek my mental training services. My phone rings like a fire alarm has gone off! In actuality, the loss is not the problem, but a symptom of something else which is behind it.

By reading and completing the *workouts* in *Tennis Inside the Zone* players, parents and coaches can follow a fun, systematic, and personally experiential approach to gain confidence in their mental game. Most players say the mental game accounts for at least 50% or more of winning tennis. Don't you owe it to yourself, your students, or your child to make the commitment and start playing *Tennis Inside the Zone*?

How will this book help you?

Tennis Inside the Zone is intended to help you uncover the mystery of the mental game. It is designed to provide you with key strategies for specific situations you encounter in competition, so that you no longer struggle with distractions, loss of focus, pressure, concentration, and prolonged blocks or slumps.

Tennis Inside the Zone will help you discover your unique strengths and make them even more potent, while identifying and moving beyond challenges and blocks which get in the way of your peak performance.

Tennis Inside the Zone can help you improve your competitive results without picking up a ball! It can help you:

- adapt and adjust during critical times in a match

- play like you do in practice during competition

- manage pressure and make better choices at crunch time

- stay focused and let go of distracting or uncontrollable events

- embrace challenges, pressure, and competition

Who should read this book?

Tennis Inside the Zone was written for all athletes of all sports, and especially targeted to tennis players. It will also serve coaches and parents, to help them understand and relate to what their player is experiencing and feeling. Additionally, it will provide valuable ideas to help them coach and support the individual player. Tennis Inside the Zone will also be helpful to anyone in performance such as actors, singers, teachers, lawyers, etc. The book provides practical value-added exercises to help athletes move forward in their journey toward achieving their personal peak performance.

Why is this book different?

Tennis Inside the Zone is an interactive experience that is designed to engage the athlete and help them create a personal experience, one which will guide them beyond self-imposed limits, expectations, and blocks. Tennis Inside the Zone will help the athlete become aware of what makes them unique and how to translate these attributes into their performance.

Tennis Inside the Zone is not written from an ivory tower; in fact I like to say it's written from the sandbox—that is, the sandbox of my clients. The chapter ideas all came from my clients!

Tennis Inside the Zone is not written in "psychobabble;" in fact it includes real examples, quotes, and stories from my clients' experiences; as well as observations from watching my clients play. For example, how many of you have said, "I'm better, how could I lose?" or, "OMG... I'm nervous, what do I do?"

Most players spend very little time on the mental game. Maybe they read an article here or there, or pick up a quote. But rarely do they apply the information to their specific situation. In all fairness, there really are not many purposeful books targeted towards junior players. This book features stories, workouts, poems, and articles which highlight specific competitive situations for the athletes.

Which direction are you going?

Ramat HaSharon, Israel Scrapbook Memory

What great fun being a guest speaker at the Israeli Tennis Centers flagship location in Ramat HaSharon, Israel.

Section 1
OFF-COURT WORKOUTS

Off-Court Workouts

To the Child Within

There's a child inside of you who holds the key to your greatest dreams.
While she may be sometimes frightened by other people and events, she
refuses to let go of those dreams.
She tugs at your leg for attention.
She whines for you to notice her.
She whispers in your ear of all that you can be.
Sometimes you'd just like her to go away with all that silliness.
No such luck. She's too persistent.
She's determined to get noticed.
She refuses to give up.
You've tried to talk some reason into her, but thankfully she won't listen.
Others have told her the "facts" and the limits on what's possible.
She's not interested in their "impossible."
She does not understand "can't."
She doesn't care if others laugh at her dreams, as long as you don't.
She wants you to consider the possibilities.
She wants to show you what she can do.
She will not quit until she's gotten your attention.
Her spirit can't be broken.
She refuses to stay down.
Her resiliency is awe inspiring.
Her enthusiasm is refreshing and boundless.
Harness that child within.
Learn to listen to her.
Let her guide you to your dreams.

— Dr. Alan Goldberg, author of *Sports Slump Busting*
and co-author of *This is Your Brain on Sports*

Workout 1
Mental Point

Athletes with the mental edge rise above adversity and adapt to what's happening in the present moment.

How Do I Get the Mental Edge?
Unlock the Mystery of the Mental Game

What the Pros Are Saying

A journey of a thousand miles starts with a single step.
> — **Chinese proverb**

There's a lot of things that can influence your state of mind. Of course, it's not always possible to be 100 per cent concentrated for three-and-a-half hours. But it's important to keep going because you fall many times, but mental strength allows you to keep going.
> — **Novak Djokovic**, ausopen.com: Mental toughness Novak's greatest weapon by Matt Trollope, 2/1/15

When you have tough times and when you learn you can't be perfect in every situation, it's hard to accept, you know, because I still do expect that. But you just have to, because, you know, it's not about the situation. It's how you deal with it. You always have a choice… Now I really try to forgive myself sometimes and to accept it and to move on."
> — **Anna Ivanovic**, NY Times: Ana Ivanovic, 2008 French Open Champion, Stays Calm in Wind by Ben Rothenberg, 6/2/15

Key Principles
1. Focus on process, not outcome.
2. It's not when you get there, it's how you get there.
3. Redefine success beyond winning and losing—play proud, compete.

How Do I Get the Mental Edge?

Ask any athlete how important the mental game is—most would say it's between 50% and 99% of competition. In individual sports like golf, running, swimming, and tennis, the value always pushes the higher limits. In team sports like baseball, basketball, lacrosse and football, it has great relevance as well. Remember Yogi Berra's famous quote, "Half of this game is 90% mental." Many athletes don't understand how to unlock the mystery of the mental game. The first step begins by asking the right questions.

Who has the mental edge? Two modern-day tennis players come to mind. These icons are Roger Federer and Rafael Nadal. These two players have been atop the men's game for the past ten years. Most importantly, they have both demonstrated their will to compete, their respect for the game, and their ability to adjust to adversity.

Similarly, the great NFL quarterback Tom Brady also comes to mind. Brady can often be observed inspiring teammates on the field, and appears generally unflappable after his own mistakes. He never seems concerned with the referee's decisions, a raucous environment in a rival stadium, or a particularly aggressive defense. He simply controls what he can, raises his intensity level when he senses his teammates need it, and works with purpose and consistency during and after practice.

What is the mental edge? Athletes with the mental edge rise above adversity and adapt to what's happening in the present moment. Other characteristics include patience, calmness under pressure, focusing on what you can control, and getting comfortable being uncomfortable. These players also have the ability to raise their level when it's needed most. Think about Pete Sampras serving his way out of a 0-40 hole. Or consider Michael Phelps, the great Olympic swimmer, before each race listening to his iPod, letting go of anxiety. At race time his mind was clear, and he performed with complete attention to the moment.

When do you need the mental edge? Performing under adversity is truly the mark of a champion. This is the time the mental edge is imperative. Most players can win when they are playing well—they have the momentum and their confidence. However, the true champions are the ones who find a way to win when they are not playing their best. Athletes with the mental edge take little for granted, give a full effort, and trust their process no matter the score or situation.

Where does the mental edge come from? The mental edge lies within each of us. It starts on the inside and can be cultivated on the outside by people and experiences. The key is to trust the process, do your best and learn from mistakes, setbacks, and obstacles. Refer to Michelangelo: he knew when he bought a block of marble that the David was inside, and chip-by-chip his masterpiece appeared for the world to see. The masterpiece already lay within the block of stone, but his genius rested in figuring how to uncover it!

Why is the mental edge important? It's the glue that holds everything together. When you have it, you exhibit flexibility in situations, accept imperfection, and work with what you have on that given day. This creates an ability to stay calm and centered under pressure. It is rare a winning performance is perfect; more often it is the "perfectly imperfect" shots and plays which change the course of a competition. A great mental approach is the most surefire way to walk into competition with an advantage.

How do I get the mental edge? This is the million-dollar question. We know that having the mental edge is a crucial component of any elite athlete's game. What many of us don't understand is that, similar to confidence and winning, the mental edge is a consequence of actions, behaviors, commitment, experience, and discipline, to name a few. Great players are very aware and trusting of themselves, their sport, and their personal process. Much like practicing your technical skill set, commit yourself to entering each practice and competition with purpose, intention, and a focus on what you can control.

Inside the Zone Graffiti Sneakers!

How Do I Get the Mental Edge?

WORKOUT

In your experience, how important is the mental game during match play?

(scale: 1 = not important; 10 = very important) _____

_____

Explain why you gave it this rating:_____

_____

_____

WHO demonstrates the mental edge? (What player or team?)_____

_____

_____

WHAT does it mean to have the mental edge?_____

_____

_____

WHEN is it necessary to have the mental edge?_____

_____

_____

WHERE does the mental edge come from?_____

_____

_____

WHY is the mental edge important?_____

_____

_____

HOW do players get the mental edge? _____
_____
_____

Understanding the above... List three actions you could do right away to improve your mental game by 5%:

1. _____

2. _____

3. _____

What would you have to sacrifice? _____
_____
_____

Is it worth it? _____   **If yes, when will you start?** _____

What specifically would change in your performance? _____
_____
_____

Imagine what it would look and feel like to play with the mental edge... Describe it.

_____
_____
_____
_____
_____
_____
_____
_____

Workout 2
Mental Point

"The foundation is the person. How you play is a manifestation of yourself. Your philosophy of self determines your philosophy of your game, including strongest and weakest points."
— Dr. David Grand

Winning Within:
The Athlete is a Person First and a Performer Second

What the Pros Are Saying

You're happy, and that helps your performances on the court.
— **Andy Murray**, *Associated Press*, 5/10/15

My greatest professional successes occurred after I had faced my most personal challenges. I used to think this was ironic; now I realize that success flows directly from having cleared those hurdles.
— **James Blake**, *Breaking Back* by James Blake with Andrew Friedman, 2007

I think it's very important to stay original, to stay yourself, true to yourself, to who you are. So I think I had to learn that and just be able to live with that and accept who I am as a person. I think it's a matter of maturity.
— **Victoria Azarenka**, *ausopen.com: Vika opens up* by Matthew Trollope, 1/24/15

Key Principles
1. The athlete is not broken nor do they need to be fixed, they need to uncover what they always could do without thinking.
2. The fruits are a result of the roots.

Winning Within

The tennis player is a person first and a performer second. This idea may seem obvious, since we are all born without a racket in our hands, and when we first walked onto the court to play we didn't miraculously change identities—we were the same person. Rafael Nadal, in his book *Rafa*, says, "Tennis is what I do; it is not who I am." Yet years later, when we hold that racket in our hands and demonstrate ability in the sport, the way others view us often begins to change the identity from person to player. Simply put, when you walk onto the court the insecurities, experiences, and traumas which you hold as a person do not go away. You carry them onto the court wherever you go. For this reason it's imperative to get your personal life in order whenever you hope to play peak performance tennis.

It can be helpful to think of your development in sports and life as a tree. A tree starts from a seed where the roots create a foundation, an anchor of sorts. The roots can be thought of as the person's values, belief system, cultural orientation, work ethic, and soul. Influential people in our lives like our parents, coaches, friends and extended family play a role in how our roots grow. For example, by encouraging such traits as moral values, personal confidence, self-belief, personal resiliency, and self-empowerment, a person will be better suited to face obstacles, setbacks, and life's challenges. Jose Higueras stated,

in the *USTA High Performance Newsletter* (Vol. 10, No. 1), "I'm a big fan of trying to make the player as independent as possible." So remember, junior players... the stronger the root system, the stronger the physical trunk and branches become.

The fruits are always a result of the roots. However, these fruits (results) often garner more attention than the roots (process). Yet make no mistake, the development of an athlete's performance all starts from the roots. Dr. David Grand, a psychotherapist and co-author of *This is Your Brain on Sports*, noted for his work in the field of sports and performance, says, "The foundation is the person—how you play is often a manifestation of yourself, including your weakest and strongest points."

Now, think back to the time you were having a bad practice or match, exhibiting bad body language, or were just not yourself. How much of this could have been a result of a rough day at school, an argument with a friend, parental expectations, or even anxiety about an upcoming tournament? Oftentimes, off-court issues and unrelated stresses affect performance on the court. Awareness of the complexity of the person-player relationship will help you realize that you're not a robot! That we are human beings who are affected by what happens in our day-to-day lives. Off-the-court stresses, experiences, and emotional and physical traumas oftentimes get suppressed in the mind, but the psychological scars oftentimes remain.

Now, can you remember walking off the court after a heartbreaking loss, dejected and rattled? It could be a match where you felt you should have won, but lost your focus and missed a huge overhead in the third set tiebreaker. You could hear the crowd gasp, as your stomach clutched with embarrassment. Certainly, the next time a big overhead comes up in a match, it's likely the image of the previously-missed overhead will flash before your eyes like a shoot-ing star. The mind and body remember.

Lastly, imagine this: The serve is a huge part of your game; in competition you tear your rota-tor cuff, undergo surgery, and have to be sidelined from the game for four months. When you return, people ask how the shoulder is. You reply like a warrior, "It feels great. Never felt better." However, in practice you're afraid to go all out and hit your bombs because of some lingering pain. Then you change your motion to

alleviate the pain. After that you go through a period of excessive double faults. What's important to understand is that the body remembers any kind of physical trauma, especially injuries and surgeries. The body will try to protect itself from further injury recurrence. Most athletes recover from injuries on a physical level, however, recovering from the mental scars is much more difficult.

Carlos Rodriguez, coach for Justine Henin, said it best in the *New York Times*: "The tennis player is still first a human being. If the human being is going good, feeling good, so will the tennis player." James Blake, in his book *Breaking Back*, said, "My greatest professional suc-cesses occurred after I faced my most personal challenges. ...I used to think that was ironic; now I realize that success flows directly from having cleared those hurdles." In summary, when an athlete steps on the court, they are still the same person and carry issues, experiences and traumas with them. The fruits are a result of the roots.

Winning Within

WORKOUT

What's your story? Tennis Journey Line

Chronologically list key moments or experiences in your past that have influenced or shaped the player you currently are. Take into account tennis or non-tennis related key moments, such as meaningful wins or losses which you learned from; interactions which may have been impactful; challenges, adversity, or obstacles which you overcame; injuries; inspirations; influences; and confidence builders. List these key moments in the order that they happened.

1. _____
2. _____
3. _____
4. _____
5. _____
6. _____
7. _____
8. _____
9. _____
10. _____

Plan your story...

Plot the 10 key moments from above along the x-axis (start with the oldest events on the left). Then rate them in terms of impact, i.e. negative or positive, on the y-axis.

Now, connect the dots to get a better picture of the ups and downs of your journey.

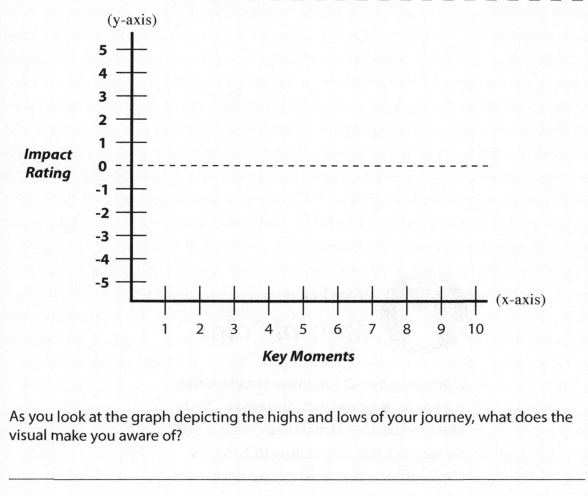

As you look at the graph depicting the highs and lows of your journey, what does the visual make you aware of?

_____

_____

Remember the times you encountered adversity... What did you learn from these experience?

_____

_____

Imagine the next five years: Describe what would you like to see.

_____

_____

_____

Workout 3
Mental Point

Becoming a champion starts with a spark, a question, a desire. This then becomes limitless desire and focus, which transcends into action, curiosity, and an uncommon passion to be the best one can be.

How to Get and Stay Motivated!
Understanding Your Big Why

What the Pros Are Saying

I never played for the money, I never played for the limelight, I just wanted to see how good I could be.
> — **Pete Sampras**, *Sampras vs. Federer: Past and Present Collide* by Tim Adams, Men's Vogue, Mar. 5, 2008

It's also great motivation, not playing just for myself but for my family.
> — **Novak Djokovic**, *CNN: Novak Djokovic: Fatherhood spurring on world No. 1* by Paul Gittings, 4/15/2015

I have proven people wrong so many times… I was told when I was younger there is no chance I will make the top 100, top 50, top 30. Every time I have proven them wrong. It's kind of nice.
> — **Caroline Wozniacki**, *NY Times: With Sense of Balance, Caroline Wozniacki Quiets Critics* by Ben Rothenberg, 9/3/14

Key Principles
1. Excellence requires uncommon passion.
2. The Big Why is the key to success.
3. The Big Why should have passion, purpose, and perseverance.

How to Get and Stay Motivated!

Understanding the best way to get motivated and stay motivated is imperative for the success of today's players. Discovering and cultivating this motivation is a crucial component of a player's development, and one of the biggest keys to the mental game. Lasting, passion-driven motivation begins with the person from the inside out, termed the "Big Why." This "Big Why" is the person's intrinsic, internally-driven reason for wanting to reach his or her goals.

Identifying and connecting to your Big Why may be the most important part in developing a player's mental game. How many times have you seen a coach working with a player who has little interest in being on the court? In this instance, the coach appears to have more energy than the player! Understanding the answer to this basic question is imperative: Why do you play? What is it about the game of tennis that you love? What are you willing to sacrifice to improve? What are your definitive goals? Whenever a player has a clearly defined Big Why, they become better able to learn from mistakes, bounce back from failure, and reach forward to achieve their goals. The Big Why is the fuel and passion that generates unyielding energy to attain the goal.

Oftentimes when doing a workshop with a group of young players, I will bring a volunteer to the front and ask them to jump as high as they can from a standing position. Each time I ask them if they can jump higher. After a few jumps the player usually says, "That's the highest I can go." I ask them if they are sure, urging the player to try once more, only to hear the resignation in their voice as they explain, "I can't go any higher." At this point, I provide some motivation by introducing a reward that is meaningful to them, proposing that if they can jump two inches higher they will get the reward. Sure enough, in the thousand times I have done this demonstration, the player always strategizes differently, has a higher level of intensity and, 99.9% of the time, the player reaches the higher mark they once thought was impossible.

After experiencing this exercise, the player immediately becomes aware of their increased motivation and sharper focus enabling them to strive higher. Now, certainly, offering a prize as motivation is short-lived and at best only provides short-term motivation. However, what is important is demonstrating how a person can achieve and accomplish more if they have an intrinsic Big Why. Furthermore, when the Big Why is theirs, they feel ownership, self-empowerment and responsibility for their performance.

Pete Sampras, winner of 14 Grand Slams, had a great Big Why, one that was personal and meaningful to him. He said, "I never played for the money, I never played for the limelight; I just wanted to see how good I could be." Interestingly, Pete was known to compete against anyone as a kid; no matter what the level, he wanted to improve and be the best he could be. Martina Navratilova once said, "To be successful at anything, you have to love what you're doing." Monica Seles backs this up by saying, "I want to play tennis for the right reason; the right reason is because I love the game." Certainly these words speak to the power of having a Big Why and drawing on it for greater motivation.

Once a player understands their goals and their Big Why for achieving them, it becomes im-portant to plan measurable and realistic process-driven strategies in order to reach those goals. During this stage the player must recognize they have choices and responsibilities in owning their success. Players should understand that they can take two roads. The first road is difficult: it requires sacrifice, hard work, and it even requires failure along the way. How-ever, the reward is a trip on "Champion's Road." The second road is easy. It requires little work, and it's a comfortable path that entails little effort. The destination of

this road is called "La-La Land." Often, I ask players to outline what each road would look like with regard to choices, actions, and behaviors in areas such as family life, schoolwork, and lastly, on the tennis court. The biggest lesson is that players realize their actions directly affect the results and they can see which road they are following: the Champion's Road or heading towards La-La Land!

Overall, the Big Why is about motivation, personal empowerment, and the power of trans-formation. It requires that players make choices and take responsibility for their actions. Cultivating the Big Why will raise a player's mental game to the next level, where concentration, awareness, and emotional management become the focus. Embracing the Big Why means rethinking motivation by putting the expectations of others to the side, and taking responsibility for their game where they can optimize their unique personal strengths and go beyond their own physical and mental expectations. Ultimately, the payoff for developing the Big Why is reaching unlimited personal potential which, in turn, impacts every area of a player's life.

How to Get and Stay Motivated!

WORKOUT

The Big Why is an athlete's key secret to success.

When an athlete has an internally-driven Big Why (reason for playing) which is not solely based on winning and losing, but an intrinsic reason which they are passionate about and which drives them... They will be more apt to persevere and focus on their process. This Big Why will enable them to strive and reach their personal peak potential.

List four reasons you enjoy playing tennis (Big Why).

1. _____

2. _____

3. _____

4. _____

Now, considering the above Big Whys, rank them in order of importance to you:

1. _____

2. _____

3. _____

4. _____

Being aware of your Big Whys, how can they help to motivate you?

_____

_____

_____

_____

By playing tennis, is there a person or group which you hope to inspire or impact? Explain:

_____

_____

_____

What "character strengths" do you get back from playing tennis?

_____

_____

_____

What's your overall goal in tennis?

_____

_____

_____

Shadow stroking your
favorite patterns can be
a great warm-up before a
match

Workout 4
Mental Point

A true competitor understands that their opponent is not an enemy but views them as a challenge, an opportunity, and a partner that is necessary to take their game to the next level.

Workout 4

Competeology
The Key to Winning

What the Pros Are Saying

I put that one (win) pretty high, because I was just really down and out… And I just feel like I just really zeroed in.

    — **Serena Williams**, *NY Times: Sparks and Words Fly as Serena Williams Upends a Rival* by Christopher Clarey, 5/30/15

I think there is inside me something … you are (trying to) reach the mountain, but you go back (fall) and you are again down. Then you fight, you go up. It's tough. You are there and go (down) again … So you keep going one metre more. You need just one meter more. When you do the step, then you feel yourself happy and proud (touching heart).

    — **Francesca Schiavone**, *rolandgarros.com: Schiavone Comes Through In A Classic* by Matt Trollope, 5/28/15

I always believed in me and try to be really consistent in my head. Sometimes your body is not right. Sometimes you don't have enough tennis. So you never know… That's why I'm happy today, because the confidence is back.

    — **Jo-Wilfried Tsonga**, *rolandgarros.com: Tsonga Dismisses Subdued Berdych To Reach Last Eight* by Kate Battersby, 5/31/15

Key Principles

1. Adapting and adjusting are key components of competing.
2. It's not whether you make mistakes, but how you rebound from them.
3. Define success based on objectives of improvement, not what the scoreboard says.

Competeology

Did you know that the suffix *-ology* means "the study of?" For example, *astrology* is the study of stars, *neurology* is the study of the nervous system, and *ideology* is the study of ideas. So what does this have to do with sports? I would like to introduce a new "-ology" into the world, one that sets the top players apart from the rest. *Competeology*—the study of competing. Understanding how to compete is the key to sustainable and long-term success in any sport.

So why is competeology so important during competition? Think of it this way: We require a basic knowledge of all the sciences to understand the world we live in; therefore, wouldn't it make sense that we require a basic knowledge of how to compete, what it means to compete, and the key tenets of competing in order to understand sports? This understanding will position a player to maximize their potential.

By successfully utilizing the below eight tenets of competing, you can earn your Ph.D. in competeology. More importantly, this applied degree will position you to unleash your potential.

1. Maintain a growth-based attitude vs. a fixed attitude: A competitor exhibits a growth attitude. They understand that their development is a process, and while a loss may hurt, there are lessons that must be learned. They see challenges and losses as an opportunity to grow, not as a problem. An athlete with a fixed mentality sees their talent as unchangeable and gets exceedingly frustrated with setbacks, as they think it's an indictment of their self-worth. A setback sends them into a tailspin, which they usually cannot climb out of. A competitor, however, possesses an opportunity-based or growth mind-set and continually puts themselves in situations where the outcome is unknown. Such a mindset creates only positive outcomes: The competitor may lose, yet know they gave a great effort and learned from the match; or they may play so well that they exceed their highest expectations.

2. Sportsmanship: A competitor respects themselves, their opponent, and the game. Their focus is on ethically following the rules while trying their best. A competitor plays with self-belief, but checks their ego at the door. This allows them to play free and adapt and adjust to situations. They don't hold on to expectations of what others think—rather, they acknowledge their opponent for putting him- or herself on the line. This mindset allows them to focus on their own game and the best tactics to utilize within the contest. A true competitor understands that their opponent is not an enemy but views them as a challenge, an opportunity, and a partner that is necessary to take their game to the next level.

3. Focus on what you can control, and let go of the rest: A competitor stays focused on what they can control: Things such as effort, energy, time management, and bouncing back from adversity—to name a few. They understand that they cannot control how well their opponent plays, court conditions, or winning and losing. When a competitor focuses on their game, utilizes their strategy, and competes to the fullest, they always walk away knowing they did their best on that day.

4. Never, ever, ever give up: Competing means never giving up. A true competitor understands that not every day is going to bring top-level performance. Such a player thrives under adversity, especially the adversity of having to figure out what to do when their game is not on. A true competitor doesn't mind winning a tight, or even ugly, contest. They have perspective; they prioritize learning from the experience over the result. Before winning the 2010 Wimbledon Championships, Rafael Nadal said, "I just try my best in every moment, every practice, every point."

5. Adapt and adjust to situations: A competitor is constantly adjusting and adapting within a contest. This is what separates the great players from the good ones. Momentum shifts are a given in a contest. What's most important is to be aware of what is happening, and adjust and adapt. Too often in the heat of competition, athletes get caught up solely on the result,

or what *was*. This singular focus takes them away from a key question: What do I need to do to play better *now*, or to get back in the match?

6. Get comfortable being uncomfortable: A competitor understands that during competition they may have to take a calculated risk, try something new, or hit a shot not quite the way they would ideally like to. They understand that they may have to navigate through momentum shifts which are not always comfortable for them. However, they also understand that by embracing the idea of getting comfortable being uncomfortable, their game will become more diverse and escalate to another level.

7. Be aware and make high percentage choices: A competitor makes high-percentage choices during all stages of their competition. For example, does a tennis player try to hit a screaming winner down the line that may appear on ESPN, or counter with a defensive shot that will get them back to a neutral position? Or does a player go for an outright winner, something they can't control, or go for target zones? Sometimes the best choice is to stay patient, stay in the point until an opportunity presents itself.

8. Learn from mistakes: Babe Ruth was noted for saying, "Every time I strike out I am one step closer to hitting a home run." What the Babe understood was that mistakes, setbacks, and failures happen. In fact they should be expected, encouraged and, most importantly, used as feedback. If we don't make mistakes, we are not pushing ourselves. Mistakes are only bad if the player does not learn from them. Mistakes provide a player the opportunity to learn and adjust, essentially correcting their mistakes from the previous setback. Mistakes are a necessary, albeit painful, part of the process of improving. Nothing great was ever achieved without adversity!

By following the above tenets of Competeology, you will put yourself in the best position to achieve optimum results. These concepts are all within a player's, or team's, control, and will therefore increase your confidence in competition. They will help you to stay present instead of worrying about results, focusing on the past, or looking ahead to the future. Lastly, they will help you become increasingly aware of what is happening, which will allow you to relax and make better decisions. Ultimately, following the tenets of Competeology will free you to learn and grow every time you compete.

This is a key to sports success!

Competeology

WORKOUT

com·pete (kəm·pēt'): 1. from late Latin competere: to strive together, meet, come together, agree; from com- [together] + petere [to seek]; 2. to enter into or be in rivalry; contend; vie (in a contest, athletic meet, etc.).

Name two players who, in your opinion, compete well.

Player #1: _____   Player #2: _____

List the characteristics, attributes, or behaviors that make them good competitors.

Player #1:   **Player #2:**

_____   _____

_____   _____

_____   _____

_____   _____

_____   _____

Is there anything on this list that the player cannot control?_____

Recognizing this, what does this mean for you?_____

Identify the top three characteristics, attributes, or behaviors from above that, if you improved, you would see the biggest results:

1. _____

2. _____

3. _____

What would happen or be different if you improved on the above things?

_____

_____

_____

 Workout 5
Mental Point

**A player needs to make a choice:
That is, to trust their training,
themselves, and their individual
process. These choices pertain to
what a player can control and what
they cannot.**

Workout 5

So You Want to Win!
What Will It Take?

What the Pros Are Saying

The fight is won or lost far away from the witnesses—behind the lines, in the gym, and out there on the road, long before I dance under those lights.

> — **Muhammad Ali**, from a poster

My theory now is to relax and play the match as best as I can. I don't have to win anymore. I can just have fun.

> — **Serena Williams**, *ausopen.com: Serena Embraces the Challenge* by Alexandra Willis, 1/29/15

You have to sacrifice and do something that's not normal, because you want to become not normal. To become a great champion, you can't do what the average Joe does. Because you're not going to get there.

> — **Eugenie Bouchard,** *NY Times Magazine, Eugenie Bouchard could be tennis next big shot* by Susan Dominus, 5/21/14

Key Principles

1. Attaining success is easier when you let go of expectations.
2. The more you "need" to win, the less you will.
3. A key question to ask yourself is: What will it take?

So You Want to Win!

When a player places too much emphasis on the outcome of winning or losing, and not "what it will take" to reach the desired outcome, they are focused on something which they cannot control (results). Effectively, they are no longer playing in the present, but in the future. When this happens, they have fallen into a trap... metaphorically speaking, one eye is focused on winning, and the other eye on the process. This creates a distracted and cross-eyed player. Optimum focus requires two eyes!

A player needs to make a choice: That is, to trust their training, themselves, and their individual process. More specifically, these choices pertain directly to what a player can control, both on and off the court. Clearly, the desire to win is definitely a goal when an athlete competes. However, this outcome-oriented focus cannot be directly controlled. Athletes put themselves in the best position to win when they play in the present instead of focusing on future outcomes (the result). As an athlete, you must open yourself to the unknown. It is here that three things can happen:

- The athlete finds they are not good enough on that day to win.

- The athlete learns what skills need to be honed for the next event.

- The athlete exceeds their wildest expectations...

How high can YOU reach?

So You Want to Win!

WORKOUT

We all want to win!

However, most people don't realize that winning is often the result of specific actions. Wanting to win is not good enough.

What's important is to understand and define what specific actions are necessary to begin the climb to put yourself in the best possible position to win.

List the actions that are necessary to put yourself in a position to compete and give yourself the best opportunity to win.

Workout 6

Mental Point

See it! Dream it! Feel it! Go for it!

Goal Setting:
Players Don't Plan to Fail, But They Do Fail to Plan

What the Pros Are Saying

I promise you, I don't get up every morning thinking about being number one, I get up thinking that I have got a match, and I need to try to play as well as I possibly can.

      — **Rafael Nadal**, *NY Times Magazine: Ripped. (Or Torn Up?)* by Cynthia Gorney, 6/17/09

You can't measure success if you have never failed. My father has taught me that if you really want to reach your goals, you can't spend any time worrying about whether you're going to win or lose. Focus only on getting better.

      — **Steffi Graf**, *Tennis: Winning the Mental Game, p. 36*, by Robert Weinberg

I think I'm on the right track. I started the year off a little slow. My results this year haven't been fantastic, but I feel like I have improved. I know I have.

      — **John Isner**, *Miami Herald: John Isner celebrates win by watching other tall athletes in NCAA tournament* by Michelle Kaufman and Bill Van Smith, 3/28/15

Key Principles
1. Goals point you in the right direction.
2. Define success based on your individual improvement, not the outcome.
3. Focus on the process, what you can affect vs. the outcome.

Goal Setting

oal setting is a key part of the mental game in tennis. Rafael Nadal, who was once referred to as the greatest #2 player in the history of the game, said this about goals: "Every morning I wake up with clear goals in my head, on how I need to improve my game. I want to become a better tennis player." By precisely following this strategy and reaching for his goals, Nadal is now, as of this writing, a twelve-time Grand Slam winner.

Think about it. If you were driving from New York to California, would you do it without a map or global positioning system? The answer is no! Without proper direction you would get lost and never reach your destination. Similarly, if you wanted to reach a ranked position in tennis, setting goals and strategies to reach them would certainly make your trip a lot less bumpy! Goals provide motivation, focus, and a clear direction for reaching the ultimate destination. Creating goals is worthwhile because it helps the player commit and focus on one thing.

Of equal importance to goals is a strategy. A strategy lays the groundwork needed to strive for the goals. Without strategy, goals will lie dormant because there is no plan to reach them. For instance, if a player's goal is to play #1 singles for their school team, they must ask themselves, "What do I need to do to reach this goal? What are the steps I need to take?"

For a goal to be important, it must be personal and meaningful to the player trying to reach it. It is important that goals be created by the player and the coach. Additionally, parents should also sign off on the goals so they can best support the process. Goals should be flexible, adjustable and revisited after an agreed-upon timetable. Often a player will exceed a goal, thus warranting the setting of another, more challenging goal. Or, conversely, when a goal is not reached, a new goal should be made to replace the goal not achieved.

Goals should be challenging and realistic. This will provide an additional focus and sense of competition in chasing them. Goals must be message-specific, so the person knows what they are chasing; and time-

specific, which will provide a sense of urgency. Goals should be written down, and can even be shared with teammates; this allows your team to help in their achievement. Lastly, goals are most meaningful when they are established for both the short and long term.

An important aspect of goal setting is determining where the player currently is in the process. A realistic and objective view will help the player become more aware of their situation, and understand what they have to do to achieve their goals.

Many people have only heard of outcome- or results-oriented goals. These goals are black and white, and fall short in key areas. This is because the player does not have complete control over outcome goals, such as winning and losing. Oftentimes a player may play a great match only to lose. Conversely, a player could play a poor match and win. Outcome- or results-oriented goals also serve to split a player's attention, since they demand that a player be focused on the result while also playing the match. Consequently, a player's full attention is not on the game. The great Pete Sampras is a perfect example of someone who decided not to get caught up in outcome goals. As a junior, he gave up his two-handed backhand in favor of a one-handed backhand. Because of this switch, his junior ranking dropped while he got up to speed—but in the long run it paid off. If he were only concerned with outcome goals, he might never have persevered though the process of the switch.

A more common type of goal, increasingly being used with today's players and in conjunction with outcome goals, is process-driven goals. These goals focus on the steps that an athlete must take in order to reach the outcome goals. While an outcome goal may be to win the match, the process goal would ask, "What do I need to do to win? What steps must I take? And, how and when must I take them?" Process goals are in the athlete's control. For example, tennis players can't control the score in the final set of a match. They can, however, control how much they prepare and practice for that moment. Process-driven goals can include running miles for endurance, returning a hundred serves with the forehand and backhand, and practicing footwork. Steffi Graf certainly shows an understanding of the process as she states, "You can't measure success if you have never failed. My father taught me that if you really want to reach your goals, you can't spend any time worrying about whether you're going to win or lose. Focus only on getting better." When an athlete focuses on process-driven goals, the result will take care of itself.

It's clear that both outcome and process-driven goals are important. I recommend that an athlete establish their outcome goals and then determine what the process goals will be to reach them. It is important to prioritize your goals, as this will help you focus on what's most important. However, as noted sport psychologist Dr. Alan Goldberg says, "Once the competition starts, the outcome goal should be parked at the door and the athlete should only focus on the moment and the process of what they need to accomplish." Another way to look at this is to let go of any outcome-related expectations and just play. Interestingly, research has confirmed that reaching process goals not only enhances performance, but also reduces anxiety and builds a sense of confidence.

Goal Setting

WORKOUT

What is a goal you want to accomplish?

_____

_____

Why is this goal meaningful to you?

_____

_____

_____

Rate, on a scale of 1-10, where you are now towards achieving this goal (10 = achieved goal).

_____

What are three steps that you must do to achieve this goal?

1. _____

2. _____

3. _____

Do you have the skills to do these?

_____

If not, what skills are necessary to develop?

_____

_____

What can you do immediately to help you reach the goal?

_____

_____

_____

_____

What can you do in the long term to reach this goal?

_____

_____

_____

In attempting to reach this goal, how hard do you think it will be?

_____

What could stop you?

_____

_____

Will you let it?_____

_____   _____

Signature   Date

Workout 7
Mental Point

Awareness and the 5 A's is a formula for problem-solving on the court, field, track, or in life. It is one of the largest components of being a good competitor. This formula is used by great leaders like Nelson Mandela, and great players like Rafael Nadal.

What Does it Take to Win?
Awareness and the 5 A's

What the Pros Are Saying

Beginnings are tough. I need to be ready to accept all the situations that's going to happen or happened and try to be strong, accepting everything, and working hard to be back the way that I want to be. When I say 'be back,' I don't mean win or lose, I mean have the feeling on court.

> — **Rafael Nadal**, *ausopen.com: Rafa Tells it Straight After Early Exit* by Alexandra Willis, 1/27/15

I tried many things… One of them was trying to put it up high. Another one was trying to chip it shorter. Another one was trying to hit through the wind. Obviously, I was not going to leave the French Open without having tried everything out there. So it was tough. Would have loved to have won the breaker, would have loved to come back in the first set, but wasn't so.

> — **Roger Federer**, *NY Times: Tsonga Scratches Out a Win, and a Roland Garros Love Note* by Ben Rothenberg, 6/2/15

Freedom is not given to us by anyone; we have to cultivate it ourselves. It is a daily practice... No one can prevent you from being aware of each step you take or each breath in and breath out.

> — **Thich Nhat Hanh**

Key Principles
1. Change starts with Awareness, Acknowledgment, Accountability, Adaptability, Adjustment, and Assessment. This becomes a never-ending circular process.
2. Only through knowing where you are can you get somewhere else.
3. Rock-bottom provides a place for a fresh start.

What Does it Take to Win?

Can you think of someone whom you consider a hero? How about Captain Sullenberger? He was the U.S. Airways captain who safely landed Flight 1549 on the Hudson River and saved the lives of 155 passengers on January 15, 2009. Now think about a great champion, such as Roger Federer. These heroes and champions have many common characteristics, such as courage, fearlessness, and calm under pressure, to name just a few. In order to be a hero or a champion, you must be able to manage adversity, embrace challenges, and be a problem solver. The Chinese have a saying—"A star shines brightest when it's in the darkest hour." In other words, when things get difficult the true champion adapts to whatever the situation needs at that time.

We often get mesmerized by the winner, lauding them with trophies and praise. Yet the most important component is to understand what it took for that victory to happen. How do they compete so hard, and so effectively? The hero or champion became that way by overcoming adversity, embracing challenge, and making the appropriate adjustments. There is another saying, that "You can't change the wind, but you can change the direction of the sails." We have all seen players continually do the same thing leading to the same results. Think about a tennis match where a player has no awareness of the opponent's strength, and continues to play to it until they walk off the court with bag in hand and head down. Or, think about a basketball team which doesn't adjust to cover a hot shooter until that player drops the last three-pointer at the buzzer. Or lastly, a pitcher who doesn't adjust to the umpire's strike zone and continually throws balls. Einstein said, "The definition of insanity is doing the same thing and expecting different results."

Probably the most important component of sports and life is the ability to be aware of a situation and adjust to it. The United States Tennis Association (USTA) states in their coaching philosophy that great players are great problem-solvers, and juniors need to be able to think for themselves in order to become great problem-solvers. In order to do this, it's imperative to have a framework in place that you are able to systematically apply to the problem. The remainder of this workout will focus on this framework, and what I believe to be the most important mental characteristics essential for improvement, success, and ultimately reaching your personal peak performance. This framework includes awareness and the five A's: acknowledgment, accountability, adjustability, adaptability, and assessment. Without this framework, a competitor will be unaware of what is unfolding in front of them; and will be unable to change and reach the results they wish for.

Awareness: The first step to solving any problem is having awareness—without being aware, a person is unable to assess and determine the current reality of a situation. It entails simply and non-judgmentally observing what is happening, being curious, and staying in the present. In sport situations, this is especially critical, as momentum and circumstances can shift in a tenth of a second. Only by being in the present can you accurately assess a situation. If you are stuck in the past, that baggage will skew your views—and similarly, if you are focused on the future, you will be unable to accurately see what is unfolding in front of you.

Acknowledgment: By acknowledging a situation, it doesn't mean you have to like it—in fact it's okay to hate it, especially if you're behind or not playing well. For example, if you are down 0-6, 0-3, by acknowledging that this is happening, you can then decide what you can do about it. Athletes often say, "Why should I acknowledge it? That implies complacency." This is not so. Acknowledgment simply means that you're aware of the current reality. In effect, I'm suggesting that this provides a choice and the opportunity to either make a change or do nothing. I once asked Mike Bryan, the famous tennis doubles player, what he did when he was nervous. He explained that he acknowledged his nerves, and changed his focus to his breathing ritual.

Accountability: If a player does not take accountability, they will blame the circumstances on someone or something else and nothing will change—and their game will certainly not improve. This attribute can be painful, but refer to this saying: "It may hurt, but the truth will set you free." Look to your own role first and foremost when dealing with defeat, and take a real inventory of what you must do to improve.

Adaptability: This refers to adapting internally to the situation that has unfolded—in other words, being able to mentally reframe a situation. Once a player can go from the negative to the neutral (or, preferably, the positive), they can change the situation towards their advantage. Internal adaptation is imperative—without this the actions will have no power, passion, or meaning. Often a player needs to change their mindset and emotional status, rather than their strategy, to earn success.

Adjustability: This refers to making changes in physical or technical strategy, based on the situation. For example, in the finals of the 2010 Australian Open, Roger Federer knew Andy Murray's backhand was strong, therefore he softly sliced to Murray's backhand. This forced Murray to hit up on the ball and to generate his own pace. Consequently, Murray's backhand was no longer a weapon. Perhaps the most famous version of adjustability was the great Muhammad Ali's recognition that he could not outfight George Foreman in their 1974 clash in Zaire. Recognizing that Foreman hit harder and had trained to cut off Ali's escape routes, Ali leaned on the ropes, taunting Foreman and allowing him to throw copious amounts of punches, largely without throwing back. By the middle of the fight Ali still stood and Foreman was running out of gas. By the eighth round Foreman collapsed in exhaustion, and Ali was again champion.

Assessment: This is continual and must be done after the athlete has made adjustments and adapted. Oftentimes a player is very close to achieving a goal, however just one or two more tweaks are needed. The adjustment step allows this. Without the assessment, it is not possible to determine the results of the previous steps. Additionally, this step allows the entire process to begin again en route to goal achievement.

Awareness and the 5 A's is a formula to problem-solving on the court, field, track, or in life. It is one of the largest components of being a good competitor. This formula is used by great leaders like Nelson Mandela, and great players like Rafael Nadal. Think about what it takes to accomplish anything significant in life. Inevitably, awareness and the 5 A's will be necessary, whether it be taking a test, winning a match, or being elected to a position. Remember, you can't be a hero (or win) unless you overcome adversity. The only way is to be aware of it, acknowledge it, be accountable, internally adapt to it, externally make the required adjustments, and then assess what has been done and get ready to begin again! Commit to these actions and you can feel good about your performance every time you compete.

What Does it Take to Win?

WORKOUT

The solution to any problem starts with awareness!

Awareness: Name a specific tennis situation that is troubling you. (describe it)

_____

Acknowledgment: What can you do to acknowledge the situation?

_____

Accountability: What can you do to take accountability for the situation?

_____

Adjustability: What can you do to physically adjust to change the situation?

_____

Adaptability: What can you do to mentally adapt to change the situation?

_____

Assessment: Based on the previous steps, how would you assess things?

_____

Workout 8
Mental Point

The gift of the body is that it is always centered and present. To move into the part of you that has the power to transform your life experiences and perform without limits, you must bring your awareness to your body, your breath, your senses.

Playing Inside the Zone:
One Point at a Time

What the Pros Are Saying

I think I played the best tennis in my life. For all the other players who work hard, this is a sign that it is going to pay off.

— **Marin Cilic**, *The Guardian: Marin Cilic crushes Kei Nishikori to win US Open and first grand slam* by Kevin Mitchell, 9/8/14

At the time, I was in a funk on the court, in a trance that I could hardly remember anything afterwards. I was in the famous zone. Suddenly everything was running on automatic. I had the feeling that I couldn't do anything wrong.

— **Roger Federer**, *Quest for Perfection*

The zone is not somewhere we go or enter, rather it is a natural state we are born in.

— **Rob Polishook**, Author

Key Principles
1. Try softer, not harder.
2. Trust yourself—the real answers are inside.
3. Remember your training—trust your instincts.

Playing Inside the Zone

The "zone" is a state of being entirely in the present, free of all distractions. A state of being that exists within each of us. Playing inside the zone requires an athlete to be aware, yet not *over-think, judge* or *over-try*. This state requires an implicit acceptance of what the athlete is experiencing at that particular time. It is a state where the athlete no longer analyzes technique but, rather, just plays, flows and competes. Paradoxically, when an athlete plays inside the zone, the result is usually well beyond expectations. The result: a smooth, harmonious, effortless flow of energy that produces a limitless performance.

These moments are also called 'peak experiences' by the humanistic psychologist Dr. Abraham Maslow, whose research shows that those who achieve these types of occurrences feel 'more integrated;' 'at one with the experience;' 'relatively egoless;' 'at the peak of his powers;' 'fully functioning;' 'in the groove;' 'free of blocks, inhibitions, cautions, fears, doubts, controls, reservations, self-criticism;' 'spontaneous and more creative;' 'in the here and now;' 'non-striving, non-needing, non-wishing... he just is.' To sum it all up: The feat being attempted is effortless, like flowing water.

As athletes, we are all capable of playing inside the zone. It is a natural state that is experienced, not invented. It is not a destination that you travel to; rather, it is a place that, when you let go of all the distractions within and stay present, will find you. This feeling is aptly addressed in the 2000 movie "The Legend of Bagger Vance," starring Will Smith as the caddy Bagger Vance and Matt Damon as the famous golfer Rannulph Junuh. Vance says to Junuh: "Inside each and every one of us is one true authentic swing... Somethin' we was born with... Somethin' that's ours and ours alone... Somethin' that can't be taught to ya or learned... Somethin' that's got to be remembered... Over time the world can rob us of that swing... It can get buried inside us under all our *wouldas* and *couldas* and *shouldas*... Some folk even forget what their swing was like... Close your eyes... feel the ball..."

Playing inside the zone is the birthright of every person; in fact, each of us has already experienced this seemingly unattainable state as a young child. Born into this world, the unassuming child breathes deeply and instinctively through his or her nose, just like the cheetah, the world's fastest land animal. We learn best when we're young, free from stress and outside distractions that pull us away from the present moment.

Taking your first steps as a child requires trust in self, determination, and trial-and-error. Most children learn to walk before their parents actually teach them. They learn through observation, natural instinct, and modeling others around them. Through this process, children learn to walk gaining confidence in the natural, instinctual learning process that operates within them. Conversely, parents watch their children's efforts with love and interest, but usually without much interference. When a child loses his or her balance and falls, the mother doesn't condemn the child as clumsy or uncoordinated; she doesn't even feel bad about the tumble. She simply notices the event and provides a kind word, support, and usually a loving gesture of encouragement. Consequently, a child's progress in learning to walk is never hindered by the idea that he or she is not doing better. If we could only treat our teenage and adult athletic endeavors— tennis, baseball, football, gymnastics, swimming, etc.—as we do a child learning to walk, we would make tremendous progress toward uninhibited improvement, playing in the zone and achieving effortless peak performance.

Michelangelo, the infamous Italian sculptor and creator of the *David*, provides a classic metaphor of focusing on the process and playing inside the zone. He sculpted the Renaissance masterpiece from 1501 to 1504. Undeterred by the challenging task of carving a statue out of a mere slab of marble, Michelangelo had a vision of the finished product; he worked under the premise that the image of *David* was already in the block of stone, a concept referred to as *disegno*. He chipped away at the stone and brought out what others could not even imagine. He saw and knew what others didn't. The marble he was chipping away was a metaphor for the

distractions, limitations, fears, anxieties, negative self-talk, and uncontrollable events that get in most people's way. Michelangelo knew *David* existed, but he had to let him appear. Similarly, our best performances are waiting to happen once we let go of distractions, fear of failure and our ego.

It can be psychologically difficult to play in the present. However, by focusing on your breath, present circumstance, and the process, present moment awareness and the zone can be uncovered. While the past can be helpful to learn from and the future represents goals to be achieved, it is imperative when performing that an athlete let go of distractions and just compete in the present moment.

The gift of the body and our senses is that it is always centered and present. To move into the part of you that has the power to transform your life experiences and perform without limits, you must bring your awareness to your body, your breath, your senses, and start at the very beginning from the inside out, much like the eye of a hurricane: still on the inside and unpredictable on the outside. Bagger Vance knew this. He said, "There's only *one* shot that's in perfect harmony with the field... One shot that's his authentic shot... there's a perfect shot out there tryin' to find each and every one of us... All we got to do is get ourselves out of its way, to let it choose us... Seek it with your hands. Don't think about it... Feel it."

Playing Inside the Zone

WORKOUT

Remember a time... when everything was flowing and you were playing Inside the Zone:

When was it?

_____

What time was it?

_____

Where was it?

_____

How old were you?

_____

What were you wearing?

_____

What was the weather?

_____

Who was watching?

_____

What did it feel like?

_____

_____

_____

What smells did you notice?

_____

What was happening?

_____

_____

_____

What sounds did you notice?

_____

What was your sense of time?

_____

What was going through your head?

_____

_____

Overall, what words or images come to mind?

_____

_____

What else do you remember about that time you were playing Inside the Zone?

_____

_____

_____

Connecting to your 'Inside the Zone' image is similar to how the top pros use their towel, bounce the ball, or perform their specific routine to help them let go and relax before beginning the next point.

How can you use your 'Inside the Zone' image to help you?

_____

_____

_____

 Workout 9

Mental Point

Imagine you achieved that sought-after goal... What would it look like? And feel like? What specific things would have had to happen?

Dream On!
How Imagery Can Help You Win

What the Pros Are Saying

Before I play a match... I visualize myself playing typical points based on my opponent's style of play... This helps me prepare mentally for a match... before I even walk on the court.
> — **Chris Evert**, *in The Mental ADvantage* by Robert Weinberg

I see one coming and visualize where I am going to hit it, and the shot's perfect—and I feel beautiful all over.
> — **Billie Jean King**, *Smart Tennis: How to Play and Win the Mental Game,* 1999

Freed from the thoughts of winning, I instantly play better. I stop thinking, start feeling. My shots become a half-second quicker, my decisions become the product of instinct rather than logic.
> — **Andre Agassi,** *Open*

Key Principles
1. Feel it, see it... do it!
2. If you can see it, you can do it.

Dream On!

What images come to mind when you hear the phrases "Once upon a time..." or "Imagine this..." or "Remember the time...?" For most of us, these words kick-start a sense of relaxation, almost as if a movie begins to play through our mind about something that once happened. If you are really in tune to yourself, the movie may play in color with surround sound. The concept of visualization is similar: creating a mental picture of the situation unfolding. However, unlike memories, imagery occurs before competition begins. Successful athletes like Jerry Rice, Chris Evert, and Michael Jordan often spoke about how they used visualization to prepare for competition. Jack Nicklaus once said, "I never hit a shot, even in practice, without having a sharp picture of it in my head. First I see the ball, where I want to finish... then see the ball going there."

This workout will highlight the different aspects of imagery: What is imagery in sport? Who is using it? When can it be used? How can it be used? And how can it help you improve your performance in competition?

Studies show that 90% of Olympic athletes use some kind of imagery in their training. Most sport psychology consultants employ imagery as a key mental skill with their athletes. Many feel it is one of the most effective methods of preparation for competition. I feel it can be extremely effective, especially when the athlete performs the imagery in real time, incorporating sight, feel, emotions, and smell. The most important component when beginning imagery is that the athlete is relaxed and in a calm state of awareness. This will facilitate relaxation and a fertile ground for the imagination to flourish.

What is imagery? Imagery is the purposeful act of rehearsing a task mentally with the intent of learning it. It incorporates all of the senses: visual, kinesthetic, auditory, tactile, and olfactory. Additionally, it involves imagination, emotion, feelings and moods. Essentially the idea is to use your imagination to create or recreate a situation in the future, which will help you to have exposure and prepare for the possible scenario which may unfold. Alternatively, it is often used to practice a skill or sequence of skills such as a serve, a dive, or gymnastics pattern. What's important is that if you can imagine it or see it, you can then have an opportunity to execute the skill or more calmly react to the situation. For example, what is a shot or movement pattern you are learning? Now, imagine yourself doing it. See it happening, notice what it would feel like. What else do you notice? Good job, that's imagery!

Who uses imagery? Successful athletes do. I suspect you have even used imagery without knowing it—it's almost impossible not to have done so at some point. Have you ever imagined receiving a present, eating your favorite food, or going out with a friend? Have you ever studied for a test where you ran scenarios through your mind, regarding the sequence to solving a problem? Most people use imagery in their day-to-day life without even knowing it. Imagine what would happen if you incorporated it into your day-to-day athletics practice with intention. If you're like most athletes, it will be beneficial.

When can imagery be used? Imagery can be used to practice a skill that the body is unable to perform yet, such as a complex movement like serving or a sequence of shots. It can be used to prepare for a situation that is likely to happen, such as 10,000 Davis Cup fans screaming against you. In the Beijing Olympics, the women's volleyball gold medalists May-Treanor and Walsh-Jennings were interviewed on TV. The interviewer asked after the match, "What was it like to have all the fans screaming and rooting against you?" They calmly replied, "Oh, I thought they were cheering for *us*!" How is that for a successful imagery reframing? That is to say, their imagery before the match had them prepared for the atmosphere to the extent that they could even pretend it was a benefit to them.

Imagery can be used when you're unable to practice due to downtime or injury. In fact, studies suggest that those who employ imagery when they cannot practice succeed more at a skill than those who don't. Further, those who practice the skill and imagery get the best results. Imagery can also be used to improve concentration, confidence and emotional self-control.

How can imagery be used? Imagery can be used in a variety of ways; included are a few ideas how athletes can use these mental skills. Cue words are often effective. For example, oftentimes in working with an athlete, we will discuss what animal they would like to play like, specifically identifying the characteristics and attributes of that animal and what the athlete would look like playing with these attributes. Because this comes from the client, they are empowered to imagine it in a way that holds much power, feeling and attitude. Other times we will work with a *situation*, imagining the feelings of what a given situation would look and feel like, then imagining the steps for a positive outcome to occur. Also, it's used to learn a specific skill, slowly going through the specific steps of the skill and how they connect. Additionally, imagery can be used to help unravel a sequence which didn't work out, and to recreate and reframe it in a positive way.

How will imagery help you to improve your performance? Imagery can help all athletes in either learning a skill or better adapting to a situation. By practicing imagery five minutes a day, you will become more comfortable with the skill or situation.

Dream On!

WORKOUT

Self-Guided Imagery Script (instructions: read the script slowly, and notice what you experience as you read the words)

Find a comfortable position... just be aware of the sounds around you, just taking them in... Notice your breathing... and just observe its natural rhythm... No need to judge yourself, your thoughts or your feelings... just notice them for the moment... let them float by... allowing yourself this moment of quiet... You may begin to notice your body slowing down... feeling your body unwind... just let it unfold... observe this natural pendulation...

Now, would it be okay to turn your attention inward... I wonder if you can take yourself to a special place... a place you feel comfortable and secure... a place we will call Inside Your zone... in this place... you're relaxed... it can be a place you have visited before... or a place you can only can go via your imagination... or it can be a place in your body, or even a feeling somewhere deep inside... that brings comfort... peace... it can be a combination of all these things... or anything... know one thing... this is your zone... and no one else's... As you look around... notice the surroundings... notice the smell... notice the feel... let it unfold... notice the sounds... sights... smells... or even tastes...

With this feeling of being inside your zone... shift your attention to the tennis court... a court of your choice... just notice what you see... let it unfold... in front of you... bring your awareness to a time you played great on the court... a time you did your best... be aware of the experience... feel it unfold... notice your energy... and your confidence... from inside YOUR zone...

What's it like to do your best... put it all on the line... play from your heart... would it be okay to stay with this feeling... even make some space for it... just notice what happens...

Now, gently bring attention back to your breathing... know you can go back to Your zone... any time you want... keep in mind you have the super player inside... you have the energy inside... use it... tap into it...

When you are ready... slowly bring yourself back... be aware of what your feet feel like touching the floor... notice the sounds around you... gently open your eyes...

How do you feel now?_____

_____

_____

_____

_____

_____

_____

Bangalore, India Scrapbook Memory

It was really cool to work with Sunil Yajaman and the KSLTA high performance kids at the site of the WTA Bangalore Open, Cubbon Park.

After the on-court workshop, I ran an off-court session which was also attended by the junior players, coaches, and the press.

THE TIMES OF INDIA

'Failure is stepping stone to success'

Section 2
PRE-MATCH WORKOUTS

Pre-Match Workouts

Inside the Zone Rap

When you're inside the zone, you feel like a king on a throne
The look in your opponent's eyes says he feeling alone
You gotta trust your instincts, remember your training
When you're playin' like this, your game be reigning

It feels like butter, you just let it flow
As it unfolds, you do nothing but grow
When your game's like this you know the feeling,
There ain't no ceiling, you're doing the dealing

No thoughts in your head, you're calm as can be
You swing like a butterfly, sting like a bee
Your movements are smooth, just like water
Playing like this, it's gonna be a slaughter

So remember the day when you did nothin' but play
You dominated the courts, served 'em on a lunch tray
When push comes to shove, you gotta play like a kid
There's so much inside you, open up the lid

By Rob Polishook, M.A., C.P.C.

Workout 10
Mental Point

**Nervousness is not bad,
nervousness is not good.
Nervousness just is... Accept it and
it usually dissolves away...**

OMG... I'm Nervous!
Five Ways to Work Through Pre-Match Jitters

What the Pros Are Saying

We are all humans... We all fall under pressure sometimes. It's completely normal, even though I have had so much experience...it's normal on this level with this kind of intensity and competitive spirit that is out there, it happens that you fail sometimes.

— **Novak Djokovic**, *atpworldtour.com: Nerves Are Normal* by ATP Staff, 3/22/15

I think we wouldn't be human if we didn't feel extra nerves.

— **Maria Sharapova**, *Tennis-X blog: I Will Do Everything I Can To End My Losing Streak To Serena And Win The Title* by Staff, 1/29/15

The fifth set is not about tennis, it's about nerves.

— **Boris Becker**, *Fifth set career records* by James Buddell, 6/1/11, ATPworldtour.com

Key Principles

1. Everyone gets nervous.
2. If you're not nervous, you're not human.
3. It's okay to be nervous.

OMG... I'm Nervous!

BZZZZ, BZZZZZ. It's usually a weekend, in my world. I may have just stepped off a court after an enjoyable morning hitting session, or finished reading the *New York Times* while eating breakfast. All is relaxed and status quo. Yet for the athlete on the other end of my buzzing cell phone, his or her world is anything but calm. Butterflies are fluttering through their stomach, their head is spinning with possible performance outcomes, and self-doubt is creeping in.

The concerned athlete wonders what is happening to them. Perhaps they are preparing to step onto the court and play someone who is seeded higher, or even much lower in a regional, sectional or national tournament. Or maybe the young player feels they need a big victory to change a recent string of bad results. No matter the situation, it can cause a level of anxiety, uncertainty, and ultimately a feeling of not having full control. It's at this very moment our paths connect with a *BZZZZ* on the cell phone, or a short but direct text message. It's always the same as I listen intently or scroll down my phone: I hear or read, "OMG! I'm nervous—what do I do???"

As a mental training coach, this is probably the most commonly asked question I receive. As many players who have experienced such jitters can attest, it's usually not the nervousness which presents a problem but all the accompanying thoughts, such as "Why am I nervous?" or "What happens if I'm still this nervous

during the match?" or even, "If I play tight, I'm going to lose." This in turn sets off another negative spiral downward, and the player's natural nervousness turns into a far more debilitating anxiety.

In light of this, I want to share five ideas with which the nervous player can gain some perspective over what's happening, and be able to better manage and work through excessive nervousness.

1. It's okay to be nervous—it's perfectly normal and natural. In fact, even the top players in the world admit to nervousness. This self-acceptance of their nerves is actually the way they manage the situation. They don't fight the tension; rather they accept it as "something inside of them is nervous." How many of you have tried to resist a feeling or a thought? What happens? It usually gets bigger and bigger, and instead looms in your mind. Remember—what you resist persists! Roger Federer said the following about nervousness: *"I get nervous quite often on big occasions, especially at Grand Slams. You wait around, you hope to get to the finals... It's really hard, it works you. You start asking yourself questions... the more you win, the more questions you ask."*

2. Nervousness is a sign that you care. Nervousness isn't bad, nervousness isn't good—it simply exists. It's your way of reacting to a situation. There are always two sides to everything, but when you're nervous, usually you only focus on the negative aspects of how you feel. However, what's the other side? Aren't you also *excited, challenged,* and *aware* of a great opportunity in front of you? The great Billie Jean King wrote a book titled <u>Pressure is a Privilege</u>. This was an acknowledgement that if you are feeling pressure, you have often put yourself in a privileged situation, such as the finals of a tournament. Similarly, if you're feeling nerves, you are usually feeling challenged. Remember to be proud of the fact that you have embraced this challenge and are attempting to succeed, and that your nerves are a simple by-product of these positive choices.

3. **If you are nervous, who else is?** When a player is nervous, their focus is usually entirely on themselves. In other words, they are not seeing the entire picture, rather just a small piece of it. Don't forget about your opponent! He or she accounts for 50% of the puzzle. In fact, that seemingly challenging figure across the net from you is very likely just as nervous as you are, perhaps even more so! He or she is trying to manage nerves and play a good match, just like you. By being aware of this point, a player can reframe their focus away from themselves and onto the entire picture.

4. **What's the worst that can happen?** Alan Goldberg, a nationally known sport psychology consultant and mentor of mine, tells the story of Greg Louganis, a famous diver who competed in the 1988 Olympics. Louganis climbed the ladder for his last dive. Knowing he needed a 10 to win the gold medal, Louganis thought to himself, "What's the worst that can happen?" His answer was, "Well, my parents will still love me, and I'll still have my friends." With this

refreshing moment of perspective, he leapt off the board and nailed a perfect 10!

5. **Why am I nervous?** When I ask this question to players, they usually say it's because "I want to win," or "I don't know how I'm going to do," or "I'm not sure how good my opponent is." Most of us have heard these responses—so much so that we accept them as rote. However, what's important to understand is that the player's focus is distracted or compromised before they walk on the court. Their focus is on something which they cannot control, which is winning (the result). More so, they are focusing on another uncontrollable, which is their opponent. With a focus on these things, there is little time to focus on what they need to do to perform their best. It's normal to be nervous, but the player falls into a trap if they become results-oriented before play has even begun.

Playing any sport requires the ability to accept and manage nerves and emotions. All great performers understand that this is a part of their process and fighting it only makes things worse. John McEnroe said, "It's not *if* you will choke, it's how you handle it when it happens." Nervousness is a natural emotion. The problem is not the nervousness that a player experiences. The issue becomes the negative reaction and fear derived from these nerves, which often lead to a downward spiral and a "frozen" player. The next time you are nervous or anxious, refer to the above five techniques to help you play your best game.

OMG... I'm Nervous!

WORKOUT

What's important to understand with nerves is that everyone gets nervous. In fact, if you're not nervous, you're probably not human! Two reasons you're nervous are that you care and that you want to do well. Certainly understandable! Further, if you're nervous... I bet your opponent is also. So... maybe it's okay to be nervous!

Remember a match where you were nervous, but everything worked out great in the end. Describe it.

_____

_____

_____

What where you feeling?

_____

_____

What did you notice about the nerves as the match went on?

_____

_____

_____

What would your experience be if you didn't judge the nervousness as good or bad?

_____

_____

_____

Tennis Inside the Zone™

Using the principles from this chapter, what could you say to yourself to manage the nervousness?

_____

_____

_____

How could you reframe your nerves in a way that could help you?

1. _____

2. _____

3. _____

How would doing the above help you in tense situations?

_____

_____

_____

Look out into the ocean...
Simply observe your breath...
Notice what you experience in
your body...

When you're nervous in a
match, it can be helpful
(between points, games or sets)
to bring up a time when you
were calm.
This mini-second break can help
calm and reset your system.

Workout 11
Mental Point

Bring your attention to your breath. For a moment... simply notice the sound of your breath, then notice the feel of your breath, then notice the rhythm of your breath. Just be curious...

How to Play in the Moment:
It's as Easy as Breathing

What the Pros Are Saying

It's pretty easy when you get nervous or get tight to start rushing and, before you know it, you don't even know what you're thinking or doing. So a lot of it is about just staying calm and making sure you're breathing and sticking to what you do best.
> — **Samantha Stosur**, AAP, Mar. 31, 2009

I cannot emphasize how big I am on using breathing exercises to stay in the process, whether my goal is winning a match or completing another task... I visualize my lungs with air, and literally put my hand on my middle to reconnect me to my body and help get me centered, integrated.
> — **Billie Jean King**, *Pressure is a Privilege*

Key Principles

1. Your breath is always in the present moment.
2. Focus on your breath—calm on the inside, aware on the outside.
3. Notice your breath and let go of everything else.

How to Play in the Moment

If you're reading this workout, you're breathing. Interestingly, the majority of us take this subtle automatic action for granted. Why is this? Breathing is regulated by our autonomic nervous system. This means it happens without our conscious awareness. This is probably fortunate, because in competition many of us would be too busy to remember to breathe! Another unique aspect of our breath, largely unknown by most athletes, is that by bringing your awareness to your breath it will calm you and help you reach that state of mind where you are focused and centered.

Our mind is usually in two places: the past and the future. When our mind is in the past, we are usually conjuring up thoughts, feelings and images of memories that have stayed with us. An example might be thinking about a missed shot from a previous game, set, or even weeks ago. When our mind is in the future, we are usually focused on expectations of what we think is going to happen. An example would be thinking about winning the match when it is 5-2 in the third set. How many of us have done that only to lose the set? Both of these scenarios are mental traps for the athlete, as both scenarios fall into the realm of what an athlete cannot control. An athlete can only control what is presently happening, therefore focusing on the present moment and point is imperative.

Fortunately, our body and breath are always in the present time. It is said that the "present" is named as such because being in the present is like a gift. The breath is one of the greatest gifts we have. When this tool is used properly in sports, it can serve as an anchor, helping us to stay centered and focused. Simply bringing our attention to the natural rhythm of our breath serves to distract us from stressful situations and focus our minds. Try this experiment. Ask yourself, "Am I breathing?" Sit silently for 30 seconds and notice what happens.

When you're focusing on something that you cannot control, such as winning or losing; what your friends, coach or parents are thinking; the weather conditions; or a future expectation, be aware that your focus is not in the present. Your focus is clearly on something out of your control (past or future). Center yourself by focusing your awareness back to your breath. While it can't guarantee you will win the next point, you will have separated from the previous stress, centered yourself, and given yourself the chance to calmly process what your next steps may be. In doing so, you have put yourself in the best possible mindset and have, consequently, prepared yourself for the next point as best you can.

The following three breathing practices can be used to guide you to stay centered, focused and in a state of calm awareness. Practice them off the court for a few minutes each day. Then, use the one that feels best for you between points, games, or any time you find yourself losing focus. You can even use different breathing practices for different situations.

1. Unguided Breathing: The object here is to bring your attention to your natural breathing, wherever it is at the present moment. Just be aware of one of the following senses: sight, sound, feel, or rhythm. How does your breath sound? How does it feel? Notice its rhythm at that moment. Don't try to change anything or judge it. Just observe its natural organic pace. You may even prompt yourself by asking, "Am I breathing?" What you will usually notice after five or ten seconds is that your breath will slow down and you will become centered and calmer.

2. Word Association Breathing: As you breathe in, say to yourself the word *relaxation* and imagine what it would "feel" like to be relaxed. Then, exhale and say the word "fear," and imagine what it would feel like to let go of the fear. Visualize the fear leaving your body, then repeat. You may make up your own words to suit the situation. However, the key is to inhale what you want and exhale what you hope to rid yourself of.

3. Rhythmic Breathing: The object here is to breathe to an established rhythm that feels best for you. What's important with this exercise is that you find a pattern that works for you and stick to it. Try inhaling

to the count of three, then holding your breath for two counts, and then exhale to the count of four beats. In fact, you may create different patterns for different situations. Have fun with it.

Whichever breathing practice you're using, once you're centered with a soft focus on your breath, allow your attention to expand and take in everything around you. Be aware of sounds, sights, and even thoughts as they pass by. Metaphorically, this breathing practice is similar to the eye of a hurricane: you are calm on the inside but very active on the outside. Jim Courier one stated, after he beat Greg Rusedski in an epic 1999 Davis Cup deciding tie match, "It was weird; I felt like I was in a hurricane. I was still on the inside but acutely aware of everything that was going on around me." This will allow you to calmly respond to the situation in front of you.

Incorporating these breathing practices between points, prior to a match, in the morning before you start your day, or anytime you feel stress, will help you approach the situation in a calmer, more instinctual and more aware state, rather than being tight and reactive. In this state you will be ready to respond to the situation vs. spiraling downward with distracting self-talk and expectations. Using your breath, you have the ability to harness its calming power by staying focused and in the present moment.

How to Play in the Moment

WORKOUT

It's as Easy as Breathing!

Breathing is regulated by our autonomic nervous system: It happens without thinking (fortunately!). By bringing attention to our breath, it helps connect us to our ever-present body.

Below are three different breathing exercises that can be used between points or games, or anytime you need to slow down, change your focus, and calm down.

Unguided Breathing Exercise

Start this exercise by asking yourself... Am I breathing? Then, simply notice your in and out breaths. One breath at a time, notice the sound, feel, and then rhythm—whichever sense you connect best with. Just be aware of that and be curious. Notice how you may let go of everything else as you do this.

Word Association Breathing Exercise

List characteristics, attributes, or emotions you would want to breathe in and breathe out.

Breathe in: **Breathe out:**

Patience   Fear

_____   _____

_____   _____

_____   _____

_____   _____

Now, as you breathe in, imagine what it would feel like to breathe patience in, to feel patience flowing through. Then imagine what it would look like to breathe fear out, and visualize the fear separating like a cloud might. Do the same thing with the words that feel right for you.

Rhythmic Breathing Exercise

Breathe in and count how many seconds the breath is... Then, notice a possible pause, then breathe out and notice how many seconds it is. Discover your rhythm. What feels best?

Beats in:_____

Beats holding breath:_____

Beats out:_____

Summary

These three breathing exercises are intended to help athletes slow down, change focus, and stay in the present. Experiment with each exercise to discover which ones you can incorporate into your pre-, during-, and post-match routines.

Look out this plane window:
- Just be curious
- Simply observe your breath
- Notice what you experience

Workout 12
Mental Point

You will find that using your mental game to change the course of a frustrating match in your favor is one of the most fulfilling experiences in the game.

Court Awareness:
Playing With Your Mental Positioning System

What the Pros Are Saying

I've just got to make sure I adjust my game according to the playing conditions here, and then we will see how far it takes me.
> — **Roger Federer**, *Associated Press*, 5/23/15

I've faced them (pressure situations) in important situations in Davis Cup, where I was putting certain amounts of pressure on myself...I think I have figured out a lot of ways to deal with it. And now it's about incorporating, and learning what it is that works for me, what I need to tell myself and what I don't need to tell myself.
> — **Milos Raonic**, *The Toronto Star: Milos Raonic's psychological game biggest challenge in Australian Open* by Stephanie Myles, 1/18/2015

> *If you want to reach a goal*
> *You have to know where you are starting from.*
> *If you don't know where you are*
> *How are you going to get somewhere?*
> *Only when you know where you are*
> *and then where you want to be...*
> *can you then figure out what you have to do to get there.*
> > — **Rob Polishook**, M.A., C.P.C., Mental Training Coach

Key Principles
1. Start with the end in mind.
2. You are where you are...
3. Change starts with being aware.

Court Awareness

In today's day and age, most people have a global positioning system (GPS) in their phone. Certainly the GPS app has made it easier to reach your destination. All that is necessary is to input the destination and *voilà!*—the GPS tells you where to go. There need be little awareness of where you currently are, and no thinking or planning is necessary. So what does this have to do with tennis? Stay with me.

Let's flash back a few years to the time when people read maps to determine how to reach a destination. There were usually three steps that were necessary: first, you needed to be aware of your current location; second, you needed to know where you wanted to go; and third, you needed to plan the most efficient route to reach your desired destination. Then, along came an invention called MapQuest. This was hailed as the greatest navigation tool ever. What made it so easy was that the driver no longer needed to plot their strategy to reach the destination—it was automatically calculated. Our fancy GPS apps not only eliminate our need to plot a strategy to reach our desired destination, but we don't even need to be aware of our current location! The GPS automatically finds us via satellite, and calculates where we need to turn to reach our destination.

On the tennis court, we can't turn to our GPS. However, thankfully all players have a similar—yet superior—tool of cognition. This tool is what I refer to as the MPS, or *Mental Positioning System*. The MPS is a human machine, run by the strongest computer in the universe—not an electronic device, but our own brain. It is activated by awareness. It requires us to examine the same three points we needed to ask when using a map, which are: where we are at this exact point in time, where we want to end up, and what the necessary steps are in order to reach that goal.

A mentally sound player can employ their MPS system in both practice and matches. When activated by awareness, the player's MPS can tell them whether they are currently using ideal strategy, what steps to take to improve tactically, and lastly, where such adjustments will lead them. In a match, it can tell you where you are, where you want to be, and how to get back on track.

Fortunately, we all have MPS devices—in fact they are hard-wired into our brains. Some players may use theirs more than others and consequently reap the benefits, while others may take the shortcuts that our GPS app uses. For example, many players simply say, "I want to win"—in other words they input the destination like with a GPS. However, on the court this shortcut will fail. The players must first be aware and able to assess the complexion of the match, patterns of play that have developed, and the score that has resulted. Once they accomplish this, they can determine what has thus far prevented the desired outcome, and move toward the steps to reach that outcome.

It is the MPS which allows Roger Federer to make adjustments at any time during a match. If Federer has failed to return serves to his backhand side after a couple games, for instance, his MPS alerts him that he may need to move back, forward, or adjust the spin on his return. Then Federer decides how he is going to accomplish this feat.

Choosing to use your MPS is a question of whether we are aware, objective, and courageous enough to admit where we are in our technical, strategic, physical or mental process. To use your MPS system properly in practice, ask yourself the following questions:

1. Where am I now on a particular element of the game?

2. Where do I want to be in a certain amount of time?

3. To get there, what do I have to do?

4. Am I willing to put in the effort to do this?

5. Who can help me?

6. How will I know when I reach this goal?

To use your MPS system in matches, ask yourself these questions:

1. What is happening at this moment?

2. What do I want to be happening?

3. What do I need to do to change things?

4. How would my position change if I made these adjustments?

5. Am I willing to make the adjustments?

Remember, when you're on the court, don't take the shortcut by trying to use your GPS. It only works in the car. Turn on your MPS system and trust yourself to objectively assess what is happening in the match or practice session, what you want to be happening, and the best strategy to effectively reach your goal/destination. You will find that using your mind to change the course of a frustrating match in your favor is one of the most fulfilling experiences in the game.

Court Awareness

WORKOUT

You can't get somewhere without being aware and knowing where you are! Try completing the following three steps in regards to a goal or challenge.

Describe where you currently are in regards to a goal or challenge. This is similar to your GPS recognizing where you are.

_____

_____

_____

_____

_____

Describe where you want to be in regards to a goal or challenge. This is similar to entering your destination address.

_____

_____

_____

_____

_____

Knowing where you are now and where you want to be... what three things do you need to do to get there? This is similar to the GPS displaying the route.

1. _____

2. _____

3. _____

Workout 13
Mental Point

In martial arts they realize that whether a competitor is practicing or in a match, it's all part of a journey where continual improvement is the goal.

Why Can't I Play Matches Like I Practice?
Five Reasons This Happens

What the Pros Are Saying

Today I was not thinking about the score, I was just going for it.
> — **Dominika Cibulkova**, *ausopen.com: Cibulkova halts Azarenka's charge* by Alexandra Willis, 1/26/15

I'll try to better deliver my shots at Roland-Garros. And if I don't win the French Open, my career will still go on. Life will continue.
> — **Rafael Nadal**, *rolandgarros.com: Smooth Progress For Nadal* by Stuart Fraser, 5/28/15

Success is a journey not a destination. The doing is usually more important than the outcome.
> — **Arthur Ashe**

Key Principles
1. Fact: a match is different than practice.
2. The more you need to win, the less you will.
3. Everyone chokes or gets tight: it's how you react to it.

Why Can't I Play Matches Like I Practice?

"**W**hy do I play better in practice than in matches? It's probably the second-most popular question I hear from players, exceeded only by some variation of "OMG, I'm nervous, what do I do?" Sometimes this question comes out as a defiant statement, where the player stubbornly says, "If I played like I did in practice, I would have killed him—the match would not have been close." Interestingly, that statement is usually true. Yet what the person is missing is that matches and practice are different from each other in intensity and pressure. Even practice matches are different, as environmental factors like fans and the stakes of a tournament are difficult to simulate.

It's interesting to note that in martial arts, they call *all levels* of competition "practice." In martial arts they realize that whether a competitor is practicing or in a match, it's all part of a journey where continual improvement is the goal. They don't look at matches as "judgment day" where a win or a loss has significance other than taking that result and learning from it. Additionally, the martial arts faction understands the expectation that practice automatically takes place within a competitive match setting, further recognizing that one's game need not be perfected going into competition. The events that take place during the competition will provide "match play practice" and lead to the development of a better overall competitor.

Rafael Nadal has often been quoted as saying that each match into the tournament, he improved and built on the previous match, much like anyone would want to do in practice. This is a very useful mindset that has clearly served him well.

Hopefully, when a player becomes aware of the difference between practice and matches, and begins to adopt the martial arts mentality wherein match play is a time to "practice," they will no longer express the frustration of performing differently—and will use this mentality to improve in match play. The remainder of this workout will explore five key reasons players usually play differently in practice and match play.

1. Loss of Focus: In matches, a player's focus is usually on the outcome rather than on the present moment. When a player focuses on the outcome, they are focusing on something they cannot control. When they focus on the present, they are in a problem-solving mode. In practice, the focus is usually on the process: learning new shots, adjusting, and experimenting with new strategies. During a match, the key is to let go of the outcome, and focus on the process of what you have to do to get the desired result.

2. Too Many Expectations: In matches a player usually expects to hit perfect shots, and shows little tolerance when this doesn't happen. Conversely, in practice a player usually expects to make mistakes and uses these mistakes to learn from. In fact, they are a vital part of improvement. In essence, the player is allowing him- or herself to make mistakes with the possible reward of experiencing breakthroughs. Paradoxically, perfection doesn't exist. Players should expect to make mistakes in matches, and make appropriate adjustments just as they would in practice. This is a vital part of the process and the challenge of competing.

3. Poor Time Management: In practice, players often rush through drills, allowing little time to incorporate rituals or even to discuss with your coach purpose, intention, and learning points for drills. It's imperative to allow for time to discuss purpose and intention on the practice court. Additionally, as a player, ensure that you take some time between shots or drills to simulate a match situation. Specifically, practice your between-point rituals. This built-in similarity to match play will help players relax and consequently play better, more strategic points.

4. Judging Self: In practice it is rare that a player is nervous. This is often because they are not judging themselves, nor is anyone else. However, in match play, judgment and nervousness almost always accompany a player. This is the result of focusing on uncontrollables such as what others think, or holding on to past points or events—to name just a couple potential issues. It's important to recognize that if you are nervous, so is your opponent! Everyone knows top players in all levels and sports get nervous. It's not a matter of avoiding nerves, but accepting the nervousness and playing anyway.

5. Trying to Impress Others: In practice, a player's focus is on improving and performing the drills that their coaches are working on with them. In matches, all of a sudden others are watching and ranking points are on the line. Players often lose track of the match and instead focus on impressing the people who are watching. Conversely, they start thinking about how their ranking will rise or fall based on the projected outcome of the match. They may also consider whether a loss to a lower-ranked competitor would "look bad," or worry about criticism from a parent or coach. In all cases the player's focus is no longer on the present, but on the uncontrollable future. It is key for a player to recognize when they lose their focus and to bring it back to the point at hand, and direct all thoughts to the present moment.

Why Can't I Play Matches Like I Practice?

WORKOUT

In martial arts they do not differentiate between practice and matches—everything is called practice. This is the same in yoga. The point is that we are always trying to improve and get better. So while match play is different from practice, what would happen if you viewed it as practice? A place to learn and get better?

List three things that you focus on in practice.

1. _____
2. _____
3. _____

When you focus on these things, what do you notice?

_____
_____
_____

List three things that you focus on in matches...

1. _____
2. _____
3. _____

When you focus on these things, what do you notice?

_____
_____
_____
_____

What is the main difference?

_____

_____

_____

_____

What things would make sense to let go of when you play matches?

_____

_____

_____

_____

What things that you focus on in practice would be helpful if you focused on them in matches?

_____

_____

_____

_____

My favorite time at the US Open Finals, around 7pm when the sun goes down.

 Workout 14
Mental Point

It's important to note, an athlete
will inevitably lose focus. Rather
than getting angry at him- or
herself, the key response is simple
awareness and acceptance. This
non-judgmental process will help
the athlete reframe their focus.

Concentrate!
Focus on What You Can Control

What the Pros Are Saying

The greatest lapses in concentration come when we allow our minds to project what is about to happen or dwell on what has already happened.
— **Dr. W. Timothy Gallwey**, *The Inner Game of Tennis*, 1974.

It was my ability to play one point at a time and not think about what just happened or what might happen. The only thing that was important was the point to be played.
— **Björn Borg**, *"Sport: The Tennis Machine,"* by B.J. Phil-lips, Time, June 30, 1980

At the beginning, I would be affected by everybody's expectations, but I came to realize that people were just projecting their own dreams onto me… I'm not a saint. I, too, am an ordinary person. I have my ups and downs. So all I can do is focus on doing my job well.
— **Li Na**, *NY Times Magazine, Li Na Tennis Rebel* by Brook Larmer, 8/22/13

Key Principles
1. The outcome is not something you can control.
2. Focusing on uncontrollables creates anxiety.
3. Everyone loses focus. The great ones recognize this and re-focus.

Concentrate!

It's happened to us all. One moment you are concentrating on playing the point—everything feels smooth, relaxed, and in control. Seemingly the next moment you find yourself in another place, feeling tense, and each step you take feels like a challenge. Add to that a stunned concern with how the match became so close, and a fear of where it is going, and your mind is now clouded over with doubt.

Or perhaps you have experienced this a different way: One moment you are leading 6-4, 5-2, and the thought comes up that you are only four points from the trophy. You begin to press, your heart rate goes up, you begin rushing, and the next thing you know you are battling in the third set, struggling just to stay even. You are left to wonder how your concentration strayed from "one point at a time" to seemingly everywhere except the present!

Concentration is one of the most important and misunderstood mental skills in an athlete's tool box. Stan Smith once said, "Good concentration separates champions from almost champions." The dictionary defines concentration in a couple ways: first, giving something your undivided attention; and second, narrowing a focus. These are well written definitions, but a bit limited for an athlete. The competitive athlete needs to create an action plan, and even more important, to apply it to the sport and the situation.

A colleague of mine, Dr. Alan Goldberg, a nationally known sports psychology consultant, says, "Concentration is the ability to focus on what's important, and let go of everything else." This definition implies that an athlete may be concentrating, but if it's on the wrong thing, it won't be helpful. Stroll by any court or field in the country, and you might hear a coach or parents prompting their players to concentrate! Firstly, the athlete probably *is* concentrating, but maybe not on the right thing. Secondly, this oft-repeated advice is not specific enough. For example, a player may be reflecting on the previous game, or anticipating what may happen in the future, while the coach is prodding them to concentrate on what's happening in the present.

Taking Dr. Goldberg's definition of concentration a step further, let's define concentration as "The choice to focus on what you can control, and let go of what you can't control." Have you ever found yourself focusing on something you had no control over? What did it do to your anxiety level? How did it affect your level of play? Focusing on something we cannot control almost always takes us off-course and creates a sense of helplessness and unease, ultimately leading to a downward spiral. Conversely, focusing on something you *can* control, such as your energy level, your attitude, and how you react to a game or match situation, will yield more confidence and sense of control over your destiny.

There is a helpful strategy which competitors can use to help them concentrate on what they can control before a match. Try this exercise: On the left side of a sheet of paper, list behaviors and strategies that you can control during a game or match, and label it "controllables." Your list might include attitude, preparation, staying positive, following a strategy, and bouncing back from adversity, to name a few things. On the right side of the paper, list what you are unable to control—such as the weather, match or facility conditions, winning or losing (you cannot directly control this or you would simply always win!), and your opponent's attitude or ability. Simply by labeling what you can and cannot control, you will have a heightened awareness of where you want your focus to be. For example, a player cannot control the wind, but they can control how they react to it, and recognize that the opponent must contend with the same challenge. Similarly, they cannot control that their opponent has a huge forehand, but they can control their strategy in the way they set up points to avoid it during crucial situations.

With an understanding of controllables and uncontrollables, it's important to note that an athlete will inevitably lose focus. Rather than getting angry at him- or herself, the key response is simple awareness and acceptance. This non-judgmental process will help the athlete reframe their focus. Without this awareness, the athlete will continue to focus on the wrong thing. During competition, the act of refocusing can be as important as maintaining your focus in the first place.

Another element of proper concentration is to understand that a strong focus on something 100% of the time is not always necessary. In fact it can be exhausting, and can even lead to burnout. Knowing when to let go, and release focus and the accompanying pressure, is a skill. This may be any time prior to, during, or after competition. For example, Roger Federer often observes what is playing on the Jumbotron between games during the match.

In summary, when viewing concentration through the lens of what you can control and what you cannot, it becomes much more manageable for the player. Further, a player can benefit from learning to refocus effectively rather than attempting to maintain a laser-like concentration at all times. Lastly, knowing that there are times when you can and should let the guard down is empowering. In fact, this letting go will perpetuate even stronger concentration by providing a more relaxed focus, and will lead to more consistent performance in every match.

Concentrate!

WORKOUT

Concentration: kan(t)·sen·'tra·shen: noun, 1964: the act or process of concentrating; the state of being concentrated; especially: direction of attention of a single object. B. to bring or direct towards a common object. To draw together and meet in a common center; to focus one's power, efforts or attention.

How would you define concentration in the context of sports?

_____

_____

_____

Inside the Zone definition of concentration: *The ability to focus on what is important, and let go of everything else.*

Translation:

      The ability to focus = The choice to focus

      on what is important = on what you can control

      and let go of everything else = and let go of what you can't control

New complete definition (write it in):

_____

_____

What percentage of the time in matches do you concentrate on what you can control?

_____

And what percentage of the time in matches do you concentrate on what you cannot control?

_____

                 Tennis Inside the Zone™

Name a time in match play when you were concentrating on the right thing:

_____

_____

What was the result?

_____

_____

_____

Name a time in match play when you were concentrating on the wrong thing:

_____

_____

What was the result?

_____

_____

_____

Understanding this new definition of concentration, and the above, how could this change things for you?

_____

_____

_____

_____

_____

 Workout 15
Mental Point

The evening before a match it is important to lay out and pack whatever you are going to need for the competition the next day. My wife, Debbie, a marathon runner, refers to this as "laying out her altar."

Rituals That Work:
Plan and Prepare for Success

What the Pros Are Saying

I took a cold shower. Freezing cold water. I do this before every match. It's the point before the point of no return. Under the cold shower I enter a new space in which I feel my power and resilience grow.
> — **Rafael Nadal**, *The Telegraph: My pre-game rituals sharpen my senses before I go into battle* by Rafael Nadal, 8/16/11

I've been doing that forever (bouncing up and down, squatting, jumping) … I have some tapes of myself when I was seven years old or six years old, and I was still doing the same. It's just part of me. It's just a great way for me to, again, focus on the next point, focus on what I need to do, not thinking about this court, the occasion, the breakpoint, the game point, whatever...
> — **Marion Bartoli**, *Sports Illustrated: Tennis Players' Endearing Quirks* by Courtney Nguyen, 8/1/13

I sometimes rented a car and drove from event to event in Europe; a road trip was a great escape from the day-to-day anxieties of playing, and it kept me from getting too lost in the tournament fun house…
> — **Patrick McEnroe**, *Hardcourt Confidential: Tales from Twenty Years in the Pro Tennis Trenches*

Key Principles
1. Rituals help an athlete feel prepared.
2. Rituals create a sense of familiarity.
3. Rituals allow the athlete control over a situation.

Rituals That Work

You can't control the future—however, you can prepare for it. I love this saying because I consider it to be an important concept to remember before a big match. Any tournament player or fan has heard about on-court rituals (see Workout 17). But what can you do 24 to 36 hours before the big match? The answer is—a lot! It is important to understand that this is not the time to make technique changes. However, this is the time that mental preparation is key.

Think of it this way—if you were a pilot, you would have a checklist of all the things you needed to double-check before takeoff. If you were a carpenter, you would "measure twice and cut once." The same goes for sports! The main goal at this point is to be relaxed so that your natural talents, skills and intuition can just flow during the competition. So, the focus must become what you need to do to clear away all the potential distractions that can get in the way before a match.

In Andre Agassi's famous autobiography *Open*, Agassi discusses how he takes great care to pack his tennis bag in advance, to the point where he knows its exact weight. This process provides him a sense of calm, as he knows he has his tools for work! The remainder of this workout will highlight key actions that should be part of *your* pre-match ritual.

1. Pre-Match Checklist and "Altar:" The evening before a match, it is important to lay out and pack whatever you are going to need for the competition the next day. My wife, Debbie, a marathon runner, refers to this as "laying out her altar." It's her process to ensure she has everything that's necessary to compete, and that she won't have to run around the day of the competition in a panic trying to find something at the last minute. Proper preparation also ensures that the day of the match you are relaxed, as it eliminates the need to complete another last-minute task. Items for the altar might include an outfit, extra shirts, socks, rewrapping rackets, extra water, etc.

2. Sleep and Hydration: Hopefully you have been banking enough sleep and hydrating yourself leading up to the match. However, it is imperative to get to bed early the evening before a match. Most adults need eight hours of sleep for a great sleep; however, kids usually need ten hours. Plan this into your evening and work backwards so you can bank enough sleep. Also, I always recommend hydrating leading up to the match and keeping water by your bed. We all dehydrate when sleeping, thus the idea is to keep that to a minimum.

3. Pre-Match Strategy and Notes: The night before or morning of a match, go through your notes about the opponent and develop a strategy. Lock it in and then visualize yourself performing the strategy in the match. You might also visualize specific situations that may come up with certain players, and imagine yourself managing the situation to your liking. It's key to understand that adversity usually rears its head during matches, be it a bad line call, unruly fans, bad weather, or the like. Preparing for uncontrollable elements and visualizing how you will handle them under pressure will better prepare you to handle the situation when it occurs.

4. Stretch and Warm-Up: This step is often overlooked. Junior players get to a match at the last minute and leave little time to stretch, jump rope, and properly prepare. Occasionally there may be unexpected events in which unfortunately a warm-up is not an option, which then makes the stretching part that much more important. The idea is to get your body warm and your mind moving, yet relaxed. One exercise that I love is to actually simulate playing your favorite point patterns without a ball.

This will get you thinking of your strategy, mentally engaged for competition, and will incorporate movement into the mix. If you watch any ice-skating event, the skaters are always simulating their routine in advance of getting on the ice.

5. Chill: So often this step is ignored, yet it is so helpful toward achieving a relaxed, balanced mindset for the match. Just before a match is not the time to be concocting new strategies or devising new technical adjustments. Look at what Michael Phelps does before a race... nothing! He listens to his iPod and just chills. He is relaxing his nervous system, so when it's game time he can give it 100%.

Utilize these five tactics to prepare for success. Proper preparation will keep you relaxed before a match, it will enable you to stay calm, and will allow you to unleash when the match starts!

Rituals That Work

WORKOUT

Pre-Match Checklist

A pilot, prior to take-off, will methodically go through a checklist to ensure the plane is properly equipped with the right supplies and will run smoothly. Similarly, a mentally ready player will go through their tennis bag and equipment to ensure everything is in order with the proper supplies for an important match. Improper preparation will immediately put you a step behind.

The first few items you cannot put in your tennis bag: rather they are intangible things that only you can control...

- A good night's sleep the nights leading up to the match, and especially the evening before (eight hours minimum)

- Drink water leading up to the tournament, to hydrate your body

- A positive, problem-solving, happy attitude

Bag Check:

1. _____   Extra racket (same kind, preferably)

2. _____   Towel

3. _____   Water

4. _____   Banana/fruit stick

5. _____   Pen, paper & notepad

6. _____   Extra clothes

7. _____   Hat/sweat bands, hair bands, etc.

8. _____   Sunglasses/suntan lotion

9. _____   Grips: Make sure rackets have clean grips

10. _____   Extra can of balls

11. _____   Something that makes you smile

12. _____   (Anything else?)

13. _____   _____

14. _____   _____

15. _____   _____

Looking out to the
Galapagos Islands.

Great Darwin quote...
How does it relate to
your tennis game?

Workout 16
Mental Point

**What if you could improve your
game by simply asking yourself—
and thoughtfully answering—a few
questions? Would that be worth it
to you?**

Stay Positive!
Seven Questions That Will Improve Your Game

What the Pros Are Saying

What is important is that my attitude was always positive. I had a winner's attitude… I was not playing at my best level, but I still maintained an excellent attitude. And if you play with a good mental attitude, even if you are not a hundred percent, you can win because, in fact, you win more with your heart, with your will power, than with anything else.

> — **Rafael Nadal**, *rolandgarros.com*, 2008

I had to spend much more time on court, in the gym, more than I would at other events. But that's what it takes to get back. There is no secret to getting the hours out there, getting the feel.

> — **Maria Sharapova**, *Sports Illustrated: Maria Sharapova heads into French Open with confidence in her clay game* by Courtney Nguyen, 5/22/15

Don't let what you can't do interfere with what you can do.

> — **John Wooden**, Basketball Hall of Famer

Key Principles

1. You can't control the future, but you can prepare for it.
2. Nothing changes unless you make it change.
3. Be curious… not furious.

Stay Positive!

How many of you take lesson after lesson, hoping to learn the latest technique that will give you the edge? And how many of you read all the key tennis publications, looking to glean one or two valuable instructional tips? Most people probably answered "yes" to these questions. But what if you could improve your game by simply asking yourself—and thoughtfully answering—a few questions? Would that be worth it to you?

In the book *Winning Ugly,* Brad Gilbert speaks about the value of identifying your strengths and ensuring that you make them the backbone of your game. With that goal in mind, I have provided seven questions below that will help you to emphasize the positive while highlighting areas for development in a purposeful, growth-oriented way.

There are always areas in which individual players and teams excel. For example, Pete Sampras would rely on his serve to get him out of jams. Steffi Graf would rely on her slice backhand to set up points. By identifying these areas, you can use them as the foundation on which to build a solid improvement plan. Additionally, by starting with a positive scenario, you are more likely to make changes, and it becomes easier to identify what is missing from the ideal picture.

Ask yourself:

1. What am I doing in my game that is working?

2. What is behind my overall success?

3. If I could imagine the ideal game—a situation for which I would strive—what would it look like?

4. What is the difference between where my game is and where I want it to be?

5. What steps do I need to take to address these issues?

6. What resources are available to help me take positive action?

7. When can I start taking action?

Stay Positive!

WORKOUT

1. **What am I doing in my game that is working?** _____

   _____

   _____

2. **What is behind my overall success?** _____

   _____

   _____

3. **If I could imagine the ideal game—a situation for which I would strive—what**

   would it look like? _____

   _____

   _____

4. **What is the difference between where my game is and where I want it to be?** ___

   _____

   _____

5. **What steps do I need to take to address these issues?** _____

   _____

   _____

6. **What resources are available to help me take positive action?** _____

   _____

   _____

7. **When can I start taking action?** _____

   _____

   _____

USTA Zonals Scrapbook Memory

USTA Zonals brings together the top ranked kids in each region across the country. I coached teams for three years in Waco Tennis

It was great fun and an honor to be selected to coach these standout kids.

Lets just say this racket had a bad day!

TENNIS INSIDE THE ZONE

Section 3
MATCH WORKOUTS

Match Workouts

Something Inside You

Not knowing if you're going to win
Is where belief and trust come in.
Belief and trust in self
And in those that believe in you.

There is never a guarantee
Mistakes will happen along the way
However the learning is part of success.
The victory is in the committing
And putting yourself on the line.

No doubt this is hard to do
Scary and uncertain.
Few are in the position to do it
Fewer do it.

However, if you choose to?
What's possible?
What could you learn?
How could you grow?
What could you accomplish?

There are no certain answers...
Along the journey
But faith, belief and trust can guide you...

Listen to that "something" inside of you...

By Rob Polishook, M.A., C.P.C.

Workout 17
Mental Point

Rituals help us to stay calm, centered and maintain a consistent level of composure. Having rituals in place helps players to manage these situations and better embrace challenges as a result.

Between-Point Rituals:
Don't Leave Home Without Them!

What the Pros Are Saying

I think for me it's just a moment within myself, whether I need to say something encouraging, whether I need to feel that I'm telling myself to keep that focus or regain the focus or change something around. It's just a few seconds. I've done it for a really long time. It helps me and I like doing it.

> — **Maria Sharapova**, *ausopen.com: Interview after semi-final win against Makarova, 1/29/15*

I obsess over my bag. I keep it meticulously organized, and I make no apologies for this anal retentiveness. The bag is my briefcase, suitcase, toolbox, lunchbox, and palette. I need it just the right way. The bag is what I carry onto the court and what I carry off, two moments when all my senses are always extra acute, so I can feel every ounce of its weight. If someone were to slip a pair of argyle socks into my tennis bag, I'd feel it. The tennis bag is a lot like your heart—you have to know what's in it at all times.

> — **Andre Agassi**, *Open*

Key Principles

1. Rituals keep you organized in what otherwise can be chaos.
2. Rituals help you stay in control and focus on what you can control.
3. Rituals should be personal and meaningful to the athlete.

Between-Point Rituals

In sports and in life, athletes are required to perform under pressure. It's part of the game. Think back to a time you experienced a high-pressure situation. How did you manage it? If asked, American swimmer Michael Phelps might recount his experience at the 2008 Olympic Games in Beijing, China. After achieving seven gold medals, Phelps tied legendary American swimmer Mark Spitz's record, which was set during the 1972 games in Munich, Germany. With the pressure on, could Phelps grab one more medal before the close of the games? If he could, he would go down in history and shatter Spitz's standing record.

Just before the race that would determine if he would surpass Spitz, Phelps stood alongside the pool. With two white wires protruding from his racing cap, he calmly listened to his iPod. It had been a common sight at the 2008 games. After all, Phelps does this before every race. What we should note, however, is that even though this particular event was an enormous opportunity, fraught with pressure for the Olympic champion, his warm-up ritual remained consistent.

Whether it's Olympic gold medals, Grand Slam titles, or even a backyard pick-up game, we are always approaching the next challenge and the pressure that goes along with it. When will the next situation occur? And how will you handle it? More importantly, what's your ritual for staying calm and present? More often than not, high-pressure situations can make us feel tense, anxious, and sometimes hesitant. But what if there were a mental-edge tool to help us prepare for the situation?

Turns out there is, and it's called a ritual. Rituals are pre-programmed processes that an athlete uses to help them stay calm, centered, and prepared for the upcoming experience. The ritual can take an athlete's mind off of the competition, help them control their pace and rhythm, and then when they return to the task at hand, they will be fresh and ready to go. Simply put, rituals create a state of control in an otherwise tense situation or environment.

Once on the court, rituals remain a valuable tool. Utilizing between-point rituals during the match will help you let go of the previous point and get yourself properly prepared for the next point.

The ritual which I teach has four stages: The first is the **acknowledgement stage.** This entails simply making yourself aware of what has already happened during the previous point. This includes the good and the bad. Once you are aware of your current situation you can then facilitate change. The second stage is your **centering stage**. Here, you should bring attention to your breathing. The purpose here is to bring your focus to the present moment, and balance your internal status with a familiar body pattern. The third stage is **strategy**. Here you decide what your options are, and the best way to approach the next point. And the last stage is the **physical ritual**. The purpose is to help you gain control with a familiar action and subsequently establish your rhythm.

The bottom line is that competition is full of pressure. Rituals help us to stay calm, centered, and to maintain a consistent level of composure. Having rituals in place helps players to manage these situations and better embrace challenges as a result. The goal of rituals is to refocus and move beyond the stress towards your goals. By creating rituals and implementing them in our preparation and performance, we bolster our physical and emotional preparedness. As a result, we increase our sense of control and level of comfort in even the most tense circumstances.

Play in the Ocean...

Who needs a court?

Improvise!

... or the Desert!

Between-Point Rituals

WORKOUT

Name a player whose ritual you like:

_____

Describe what their ritual looks like:

_____

_____

_____

How do you think it's helpful to them?

_____

_____

_____

How could a ritual be helpful to you?

_____

_____

_____

_____

_____

_____

_____

_____

Tennis Inside the Zone™

Create Your Own Unique Between-Point Ritual

4 Step Between Point Ritual		What does it mean?		What is the purpose?
1. Acknowledgement Step…	➡	Be aware of what happened	➡	To facilitate change
What do you notice when you acknowledge the previous point without judgement?				
2. Centering Step	➡	Bring your attention to your breathing	➡	To be grounded in the present moment
What can you do to center yourself (hint: breathing)? What other things could you do?				
3. Strategy/Planning Step…	➡	Decide what your best options are	➡	To have a plan going into the next point
What might be an example of a strategy if you are returning? Serving?				
4. Physical Ritual Step	➡	Get comfortable with a familiar action	➡	To establish your rhythm
What does your physical ritual look like before you serve?				

Workout 18
Mental Point

Here is the good news! We are all born in the present, and have the ability to stay in it and play in it.

Tense, Nervous... Can't Relax?
Five Ways to Manage Pressure

What the Pros Are Saying

See what nerves can do to a player... one minute you're a genius and the next you can't even find the court.
> — **John McEnroe**, NBC, Sept. 1, 2008

We all choke. That's all right. We're not machines. What you have to learn is to accept the fact and not panic. It's the panic that loses you the matches, not the nerves.
> — **Rod Laver**, *Open Tennis: The First Twenty Years* by Richard Evans, 1988

I think we all get nervous; it's part of being a professional athlete... It's just a matter of how you control them.
> — **Jelena Jankovic**, *NY Times: Simona Halep Topples Jelena Jankovic* by Ben Rothenberg, 3/22/15

Key Principles
1. Everyone feels fear. It's what you do with it that counts.
2. Pressure isn't bad, it just is.
3. If it were easy, everybody would be doing it.

How many times have you heard that the secret to playing your best is being in the present? Have you ever experienced that "zone"-like time? Conversely, how many times have you experienced being outside of the zone, where your thoughts were focused on the past, the future or even others' expectations of you? We all have. For example, you might be preparing to receive a serve and you're still thinking about how you were broken in the last game. Or maybe your mind keeps returning to a questionable line call that your opponent made a few games ago. Have you ever caught yourself playing in the future, where after winning the first three games, your mind travels to the idea that this is going to be an easy match? In fact, you think you're going to win it 6-0, 6-0! Sure enough, in all three cases, by being in the past or in the future, the results are usually catastrophic. Why is this? It's actually pretty easy to understand. If you're playing in the past or the future you have one eye on something you can't control and the other on the match. Certainly this is no recipe for success! With your attention divided, your play can only be sub-par.

So the bigger question becomes: What are some things you can do to help yourself focus on the present task at hand while you're practicing and competing? Once you become aware that your focus is in the wrong place, what are some pressure-release practices that you can use to calm yourself, get centered, and simultaneously bring yourself back to the present moment?

Here is the good news! We are all born in the present, and have the ability to stay in it and play in it. However, it does take discipline, awareness, and the desire to let go of counter-productive thoughts, such as those you might experience from a game ending double fault. Interestingly, sometimes change is more frightening to a player than continuing to spiral out of control. How often have you witnessed a player with that "deer in the headlights" look, letting the match slip away point by point without any attempt to change tactics? Hence the saying, "it may feel good to swim with an anchor, but the weight of it is going to constantly drag you down."

It is helpful for a player to use pressure-release practices (PRP) in tight situations and when things seem to be going south or getting out of control. These PRPs are designed to take your mind off of the fearful or anxious situation and refocus your attention on the present. In this refocused state, you can calmly focus on what needs to get done with regard to changing course and playing the next point by using your natural instinctual game, instead of over-thinking about technique, the past, or the future.

The following are five pressure-release practices. You will notice they are called practices, not strategies or techniques. This is because they are meant to be practiced both on and off the court. By practicing them, they will become familiar to you and will enable you to access a sense of calmness in a quicker and deeper fashion. One of my clients explained to me that when she brought her focus to her breath, at first it took a minute or so to calm herself. However, as she practiced the routine before bed each night, she reached a place where as soon as she asked herself, "Am I breathing?" it triggered a calming response.

1. Routine: Routines can be very effective for athletes. They are comfortable and consistent, and provide the player a sense of control and familiarity. There is little left to chance, allowing for a more singular focus. Serious athletes should create a routine that they can practice the evening before matches. This might include a familiar meal routine, preparing the equipment, and some relaxation exercises to help them prepare for the match instead of stressing about it. Another recommended routine is deciding what to do between points. This may include some breath work (described in practice 2, below); designating an area on the court that serves as a positive space; or recalling an inspirational moment where you had success in a previous situation.

2. Breathing: I strongly advocate using your breath as a centering and calming practice. By bringing your attention to your breath and noticing its sound, feel, or rhythm, you will automatically bring yourself to the present moment. The simple act of doing this, of even asking yourself, "Am I breathing?" will take your mind off

the pressure, help you release, and bring your attention to the present. There are many different breathing techniques from which to choose. Find one that you're most comfortable with. The key here is that your breath is always in the present; attaching to it will help you detach from the stress, create a sense of calm, and put you in the best position to play the next point.

3. Anchors: An anchor is something to which you can bring your attention, such as a memory, an inspiration, or a designated place on the court that's calming. The key to this practice is that the anchor brings about positive and safe feelings. It may be the feeling of hanging around the beach, or being with a certain someone. The idea is that this anchor is connected to a feeling that facilitates a sense of calm in your body. For instance, the thought of the ocean is often very calming for people. Focusing on this often helps a player let go, release pressure, and center themselves. Your anchor should be personal to you, and just the thought or vision of it should lead to a sense of warmth, calm, and safety.

4. Be curious, not furious: This one may sound funny, but just the act of being curious puts you in the present without any preconceived judgments. Being curious creates a sense of awareness of what is happening around you, without thoughts of the past or future getting in the way. Try this. Be curious about your opponent's game without making judgments. What will happen is that you will begin to see patterns emerge. You will see your opponent's weaknesses and strengths in a way that would not have been possible before, because now you are choosing not to label them or block your awareness with anger. Next time, instead of being angry or even ecstatic at the result, be curious about what happened. When you are curious, you usually become more in tune and open to what is going on around you. You will also find yourself becoming less judgmental of the situation at hand, which then allows you to respond in a calmer fashion, rather than merely reacting quickly.

5. Read the ball: This is a practice that you can do to help you stay present during an actual point. By doing this you will probably become acutely aware of the rhythm of the point and the opportunities to be offensive, defensive, or stay neutral. Try this: During a point, bring your awareness to the ball's spin, its speed, its depth, and the arc or angle of the shot. By being acutely aware of these elements, you will have less time to plan and preconceive what your next shot should be.

Although having less time to plan your next shot may sound like a negative, it's not. You may be surprised by how adept your game can be when utilizing your instincts connected with tracking the ball. Of course, your next shot will be in response to your opponent's, after you completely understand their ball. How many times have you had a preconceived idea that you would hit a topspin return, and instead your opponent forces you out wide with a serve? Out goes the idea of a topspin forehand. Because you had a preconceived shot, were you able to block the serve back deep? By letting go of preconceived notions, you are able to simply play the shot your opponent gives you. This practice is similar to listening first and then responding. Only by understanding what the person is saying, or what the opponent's ball is saying, can you optimally respond.

This technique provides you the freedom and flexibility to respond to the situation and not overplay a point. It relies on the athlete's ability to let go and play based on instinct, trust and their feel for the game. This practice protects against the inclination to control, overthink, and get caught up in what shot to play next. Rather, the player must remember their training and trust their instincts.

Try these pressure release strategies; see which ones work best for you. The key to all the practices is that they allow you to move away from the stressful situation and offer a sense of calm in return. Once you have attained the calming effect, you can then bring your attention back to the match and you will be able to strategize in a clear and directed manner. Remember, these are called *practices* for a reason: that means you can practice them every day for a few minutes. Over time they will become as comfortable and familiar as a glove when you use them on the court.

Tense, Nervous... Can't Relax?

WORKOUT

In this chapter, I have addressed ideas that can help you slow down, change your focus, and relax during tense situations (routines, breathing, anchors).

Let's briefly explore what can happen in a tense situation. Oftentimes a player will describe their heart speeding up, not feeling certain parts of their body, trembling or shaking and generally feeling inclined to speed things up. On the other hand, players in the zone describe it as relaxed, time slowing down, and moving to the ball effortlessly.

Our energy goes up and then naturally comes down like a wave in the ocean, that is unless a fear, anxiety, or situation threatens us and we spike up (freeze). What is important to understand is that the thought is not the problem; it's when we react to the thought. For example, I missed that shot, then taking it a step further to mean I'm going to lose.

When fears and anxiety enter your mind, practice not reacting to the fear, but rather just being curious to it. Not adding anything to the emotion, just be aware of it. Usually it will go away.

<u>Anchoring Exercise:</u>

Step 1: Think of a time or experience in a match where you faced adversity but overcame it. Describe it.

_____

_____

_____

_____

Step 2: When you think of it, notice how you feel. Describe it.

_____

_____

_____

_____

Step 3: Imagine a situation in the future which may make you feel tight or nervous. Describe it.

_____

_____

_____

_____

Step 4: Now, imagine the time from Step 1 where you turned things around, just noticing that centered, competent feeling...

Step 5: What do you notice?

_____

_____

_____

_____

Now, go back to the future situation that makes you nervous. You may notice that by changing the focus to a feeling of accomplishment (overcoming adversity), the nervousness of the future event may subside and not be as intense as before.

New York's Riverside Clay Tennis Association's red clay courts has got it right!

Workout 19
Mental Point

**Effectively managing pressure
is a counterintuitive process.
Rather than ignoring the pressure,
it's necessary to accept it. This
acceptance neutralizes it or takes
the edge off.**

Tension, Tears, and Twitches:
The Secret to Managing Stress

What the Pros Are Saying

In the past I was playing not to make mistakes... I was waiting for solutions from my coach, my husband, and a lot of other people around me. But when you're on the court you have to take your own responsibilities.

> — **Justin Henin**, *Daily Mail*, Jun. 18, 2005

I promise you, I don't get up every morning thinking about being number one, I get up thinking that I have got a match, and I need to try to play as well as I possibly can.

> — **Rafael Nadal**, *"Ripped. (Or Torn Up?)"* by Cynthia Gorney, *New York Times Magazine*, Jun. 17, 2009

Key Principles

1. Everyone get nervous; it's how you manage it.
2. Just be You.
3. When tense, slow down and notice your breath.

Tension, Tears, and Twitches

How many of you get nervous before a critical point in a match? How many of you can feel the pressure when serving to close out a match? Nerves play a key part in tennis, golf, and indeed any sport. Nerves will make a player tight: physiologically the athlete will get a surge of adrenaline in their central nervous system, their heartbeat pounds like a drum, beads of sweat start forming on their skin, their breath gets short and shallow, their muscles contract, and their blood pressure increases.

A common misconception is that the top players don't feel nerves, tension, anxiety or fear. John McEnroe says, "Everybody chokes—it's just a matter of how you deal with it." However, there are mental skills that great players utilize to thrive despite such emotions. These players are able to effectively accept these emotions as part of their individual process, and consequently release them so they can play in a relaxed state of focused awareness. How many times have you heard a player say, "If only I wasn't nervous, it would have been a different score!" or, "If only I didn't choke with the lead I would have won!" The reality is that you can't separate the mental game from the tactical, technical, and strategic game. It's a critical component, especially in high-pressure situations, and the top pros know it.

Effectively managing pressure is a counter-intuitive process. Rather than ignoring the pressure, it's necessary to accept it. This acceptance neutralizes it or takes the edge off. This is much like the well-known "elephant in the room" scenario we all encounter at one time or another. Rejecting, ignoring, or denying that the elephant exists simply leads to greater and greater discomfort. Only upon the acknowledgement that a situation (in this case, the existence of stress) exists in the mind are we able to reduce the tension.

Media, fans, coaches, and even players often misunderstand nerves and how to manage them. It's common to hear a statement such as, "Champions don't like to admit to nerves." In many cases this may be accurate, but it seems that some elite players are not afraid to express how they experience their emotions. Roger Federer, in his 2010 Australian Open victory speech, admitted to feeling "a little nervous." In fact, during his epic 2009 Wimbledon final against Andy Roddick, he said, "I used to get nervous when a friend would come to watch me play as a kid, and then it was my parents, and then it was the legends and people who meant something. Today it's okay—anyone can watch me play. But today with Pete [Sampras], when he walked in and I saw him for the first time, I did get more nervous actually."

In the 2010 Australian Open finals, the media suggested that Andy Murray's jaw tightening was a sign of a fragile emotional state. No doubt this was a sign of tension; however, the twitches were an instinctual way for Murray to try to release the tension. In actuality, Murray's nervous mouth-twitch is no different than when Rafael Nadal pulls at his shorts before most points. It's simply an instinctual—or in Nadal's case habitual—way of trying to manage and release stress.

Professionals and juniors alike are too often discouraged from being honest about their emotions, and are consequently compelled to fight an internal battle to deny what they are feeling. Mind you, it's one thing to openly publicize your nervousness to your opponent, but the real trouble comes when an athlete does not privately allow themselves to acknowledge what they are already experiencing. When the athlete fights the emotion, their focus stays on the emotional state (inducing concern or panic over what they are suppressing), rather than accepting it for what it is and making the choice to move on. Resisting an emotion's existence only makes it stronger.

One of the things that makes Federer so amazing is that he is not afraid to show his humanity. For example, remember when Federer broke down after losing to Rafael Nadal in the finals of the 2009 Australian Open? Many fans and media didn't know what to do with Federer's outburst. Some thought he was a baby, and others thought he shouldn't show his emotions like this, lest it be a sign of weakness. In reality, all Federer did was release his emotions. He even blurted out, "This is killing me." Such a revealing statement is somewhat rare in modern sports, and it was profoundly honest. We should remember that crying is one of the most instinctual releases humans have, and in this case it allowed Federer to begin the mourning process and move on. Certainly, his results in the proceeding Grand Slams, especially the French Open (where he had never won before), point to this successful reaction.

Behind Andy Murray's choked tears and sniffles following his loss in the 2010 Australian Open finals, he quipped, "It's a shame, I can cry like Roger, but I can't play like him." Hopefully Murray will realize that Federer's crying is part of his instinctual personal process which helped him release the mixed emotions he had stored up—the emotions that he couldn't put into words. Similarly, it illustrates in color Federer's intense competitiveness, and his fearlessness to show his emotions.

In conclusion, the machine-like mentality that many people have regarding nerves is misdirected. In fact, it pushes athletes farther from peak performance because they are scared to be themselves, to fully acknowledge their own mental and emotional experience. Great athletes instinctively understand a key mental edge secret—that it's okay to have nerves. In fact, accepting the experience of acknowledging tension is the first step towards releasing it.

Tension, Tears, and Twitches

WORKOUT

The Secret to Managing Stress

It's pretty easy when you get nervous or get tight to start rushing and, before you know it, you don't even know what you're thinking or doing. But a lot of it is about just staying calm and making sure you're breathing and sticking to what you do best.

— Samantha Stosur

When was a time you were feeling stressed or nervous on the court?

_____

Does this happen often?

_____

What did you do?

_____

_____

What are some things you could do to help release the tension and re-focus? Hint: Refer to previous chapters for more pressure-release practices; i.e. breathing.

1. _____

2. _____

3. _____

4. _____

5. _____

How could this help you?

_____

_____

_____

Imagine this - a court
without lines or a net... How
would you play?

Workout 20
Mental Point

The best players in the world have doubts and fears, and get nervous, just like us. It happens to everyone. The question becomes how you will respond, play through it, and avoid the negative downward spiral.

I SUCK!
How to Tame Negative Self-Talk

What the Pros Are Saying

There are lessons that one can learn out there all by yourself on the tennis court: There are no substitutions, no time outs and no coaches. You have to really learn to depend on yourself, you have to learn to become self-sufficient. You have to learn how to make instantaneous decisions that are going to affect the result of the rest of that match. Life is like that.

> — **Arthur Ashe**, *"Legacy of Ashe Receives a Breath of New Life,"* by William C. Rhoden, New York Times, Feb. 10, 2007

When I was younger, I banged racquets, but mostly what I would do was talk non-stop, putting myself down, just rubbish.

> — **Milos Raonic**, *atpworldtour.com, The Missile Finds Its Mark* by Joel Drucker, 8/3/11

There have been times in my career where people have said, 'You have to be less emotional on court'. But actually it takes more energy for me to stop than just to let it out. I do get excited. It's part of my personality, and I love it."

> — **Ana Ivanovic**, *rolandgarros.com: Ivanovic At Long Last Into The Quarters Again* by Kate Battersby, 5/31/15

Key Principles
1. Look at what's happening, not what happened.
2. Negative self-talk comes from a part of you that is scared.
3. The secret to managing self-talk is to notice it, but not get caught up in it.

I SUCK!

All competitive players recognize negative self-thoughts. It starts with that devilish little voice in our head which raises doubts, fears, and questions about our ability to perform. The little voice usually comes during the most pressure-packed times in a match. It's that voice that says, "I suck! I'm pathetic!" after a missed approach shot, or, "How could you do that again?" after another wide backhand. It's that cynical little voice that whispers, "If you double fault again, you're going to lose this match," or, "I wonder what my friends and parents are thinking now," after you flub an easy overhead. Negative self-thoughts precede negative self-talk, and without the proper awareness, they can bring even the most competitive player down.

When a player chooses to listen to their negative self-thoughts and begins self-talk, that's when the downward spiral usually begins. It often looks something like this: A player misses a ball which they expected to hit without fail, and in their head the little voice of doubt enters and begins chiming in. Simultaneously, their body starts to get tight. Instead of moving to the next point, stepping away from the line, or any other form of refocusing, the verbal self-talk begins and the player continues to harp on the past, verbally berating themselves. All this leads to tight muscles, loss of feel, and further errors.

What's important to understand is that we have a choice regarding whether to react or respond to our negative self-thoughts. When we react to this devilish little voice with defensiveness and deny its existence, the voice gets louder and louder. There is a saying—"What you resist persists." In other words, by trying to deny this voice or feeling, it only wants to be heard even more. It's also important to understand that just because you conjured up this negative self-thought doesn't mean that thought is true. For example, have you ever been at the brink of losing a match, and had a negative self-thought, like "It's over; I'm going to lose," only to bounce back? This is because you accepted this thought, not as true or false, or as a validation of anything, but just non-judgmentally. As a result, the thought just faded away and you were able to play the point like any other.

So what can a player do when they get bombarded with negative self-thoughts, especially in the thick of a tight match when under pressure? If the player is aware of the self-thoughts and the patterns, they can make the choice to step away and change their focus. Following are six practices you can use when negative self-thoughts start creeping into your head, and negative self-talk begins to come out of your mouth.

1. Be aware, and watch it dissolve away: The problem is not the self-thoughts—those are normal. Don't resist it, or fight with it. Instead, simply understand that it's a by-product of being in a high-pressure situation. With awareness of the self-thoughts, take a step back, bring your attention to your breath, and visualize the self-thoughts being released with your exhalation.

2. Welcome and normalize: Say "hello" to the self-thoughts—by acknowledging them, you normalize them. You can actually say to these self-thoughts, "Hey, thanks for sharing your concerns, but I'm in the middle of a match. Go back to the bleachers." You might also pretend that your favorite comedian is mimicking this reply, which may bring humor to the situation.

3. Put a time lid on it: Here again, the concept of acceptance comes through. If you find yourself muttering "I stink" after a shot or game, rephrase that by saying, "I stunk on that shot," or, "That was one bad game." Even after a match, many times a kid will come off the court sullen and saying, "I suck." While ideally the young player would not feel this way to begin with, a realistic and far healthier approach would be, "I may have sucked today, but tomorrow is another day."

4. Reframe the situation: Imagine that it's match point, and you're ready to serve. The thought comes up: "Uh oh, I'm so nervous." Ask yourself: What's another way of looking at this? How about considering the opportunity to hit a great serve to win the match? Instead of dwelling on the obstacles associated with our nerves, we can shift attention to the process that entails what we must do to overcome them.

5. Change your focus: You hear those self-thoughts: it feels like you're about to be swallowed up by a wave. This is the time to change your focus. Bring your attention to your strings or your breath, and just be curious. This five-second distraction is usually enough to help you calm down and regain your concentration.

6. Towel off: The towel is a great reason and excuse to take a moment to regroup. It provides a break from the action, and a time to just let go. Today's players are always being followed by a ball boy with a towel in their hand, and it isn't just to mop up sweat!

In summary, we all have negative self-thoughts, yet when you sense them escalating to self-talk, you need to regain control of the situation. The best players in the world have doubts, fears, and get nervous, just like us. It happens to everyone. The question becomes how you will respond, play through it, and avoid the negative spiral downward. When in doubt, go back to the six practices when working with self-thoughts.

I SUCK!

WORKOUT

The Art of Talking to Yourself!

We all talk to ourselves... you know that little inner judgmental critic that says "you shoulda done this," or "you coulda done that." Sometimes the critic even calls you names! "I'm an idiot" or "I can't believe you did that!"

Can you recall a match when you were highly frustrated?_____

Describe the situation:

_____

_____

_____

With that match in mind, list all the negative things you thought or said aloud. (Be honest!)

1. _____

2. _____

3. _____

4. _____

5. _____

Looking at this list, what does it make you aware of?

_____

_____

How did saying these things affect your confidence and performance?

_____

_____

_____

Would you say these things to your best friend? _____

Why not?

_____

_____

What could you do to bounce back from the mistakes?

1. _____

2. _____

3. _____

How would this be helpful?

_____

_____

_____

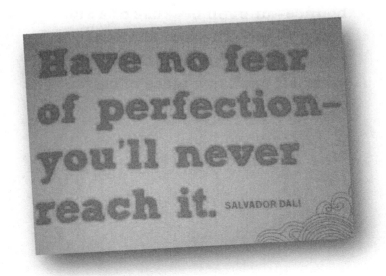

Have no fear of perfection—you'll never reach it. SALVADOR DALI

 Workout 21
Mental Point

How many of you can recall a time you were on the court and lost your focus due to a bad line call, a bad bounce—or even because of a shot you missed? The real challenge is regaining your focus and bringing yourself back to a place of calm.

You Cannot Be Serious!
Seven Tools to Help You Regain Your Focus

What the Pros Are Saying

I managed to regroup, managed to overcome that frustration of handing that tiebreak to him. It's important to regroup, bounce back, and focus on the next one.

> — **Novak Djokovic**, *NY Times: Novak Djokovic Outlasts Roger Federer to Retain Title* by Ben Rothenberg, 3/22/15

It's this moment. It doesn't matter what happens after…Whatever happened has already happened. It's about now. Now is a new moment. Let's go from here. Let's fight..

> — **Irina Falconi**, *NY Times: Out of the Loop at the French Open, and Liking It That Way* by Christopher Clarey, 5/26/15

Focus on getting better. There are a lot of ways you can win when you're young. You need to make sure that you're understanding how the game is won on a professional level. And keep pushing forward.

> — **Andre Agassi**, *Tennis Channel*

Key Principles

1. Expect the unexpected.
2. Concentrating 100% of the time is not important. Understanding when you lose your concentration and bringing it back to the task at hand is.
3. The most important moment is the NEXT moment.

You Cannot Be Serious!

"**Y**ou can't be serious, man! You **cannot** be serious! That ball was on the line. How can you call that out? You guys are the absolute pits of the world!" These were the words spit from John McEnroe's mouth as he went into his most infamous mental tirade. Do you remember? If not, simply type in "you cannot be serious" and "McEnroe" in YouTube and the incident will appear. The time was 1981 and McEnroe was playing Tom Gullikson in a first-round match at Wimbledon, when he lost the match and his focus.

Now, it's one thing to see a professional lose their focus. However, the question is, how many of you can recall a time you were on the court and lost your focus due to a bad line call, a bad bounce—or, even because of a shot you missed that you thought would be as easy as throwing a seashell into the ocean? The real challenge is regaining your focus and bringing yourself back to a place of calm where you're able to play the next point free of distractions.

It is important to understand that you must be aware of having lost your focus in the first place! It sounds simple, even obvious. Only when you recognize the slippery slope of potential self-destruction are you able then to rebound. The slope is much like the action of dominos falling, gaining momentum as they go. With awareness you can choose to respond to the adverse situation by slowing down and making the

choice to re-focus. Be aware that it takes courage to change your focus from where you were and reach a place of calm. In tough situations, try using the following tools to regain your focus or stay on track:

1. Rituals. The power of rituals lies in the fact that they are predictable actions that a player can rely on to feel more comfortable during an unpredictable situation. For this reason, rituals will help to bring you back to a place of calm. Novak Djokovic's infamous ritual of bouncing the ball prior to serving helps him to feel calm and relaxed. Rafael Nadal sets up his water bottles in a systematic manner so he knows exactly where things are; this action makes him feel comfortable and in control. Rituals focus our attention on the "here and now" during a match.

2. Self-coaching. With self-coaching, players ask themselves questions that result in physiological responses. For example, there are a number of questions you can ask yourself, such as, "If I were relaxed, how would I feel?" or, "If I were having fun, what would it feel like?" Inevitably, your body's natural physiological response will be to release tension, become curious and return to the present moment.

3. Reframing thoughts. Much like self-coaching, reframing your thoughts requires that you assess the immediate situation and employ alternative techniques to help you stay calm. For example, you may find yourself saying, "Oh my gosh, here we go again! I always screw up. I'm going to double-fault." Rather than fighting these thoughts, try reframing them. You can say something like: "I hear you, but now is the time to concentrate," or, "Yeah, this is a pressure-packed moment, so hang on for the ride." Remember, it is okay to be nervous—it's even natural. All pros admit to having nerves. However, the champions are the ones who accept the anxiety as a reality and then continue playing rather than suppressing their nerves and freezing up.

4. Anchors. Before a match, create an anchor: choose something that makes you feel calm. It might be a song, the feeling of relaxing at the beach, or the emotions you feel when with a loved one. When things get rough during the match, focus on recalling the sounds, sights, and feelings you associate with that anchor. By allowing yourself this mental break, you return to the match with a fresh outlook on the game.

5. Cue cards. Before the match, prepare a cue card with a few pertinent words, phrases, or quotes that may help you relax. Write statements on the card, such as "My opponent is my partner, not my enemy;" "Focus on targets, not winners;" "I don't have to be perfect;" or, simply, "Breathe." Then, attach the cue card to the corner of your towel. Refer to the ideas on this card during odd-game changeovers for inspiration and a feeling of calm.

6. Breathing. Bring your attention to your breath—the body and the breath are always in the present moment. By simply noticing your breath's natural rhythm, either the sound or the feel of it, you will bring yourself into the present and calm will usually follow. Sometimes noticing your breath can be too tricky or passive an activity for some players, and they become impatient. If this happens to you, remember to breathe in relaxation and breathe out stress. Say or think the words as you do this. Another breathing exercise is to inhale to the count of three and exhale to the count of four. You might even discover your own breathing rhythm when you hit the ball.

7. Eye-of-the-hurricane focusing. To use eye-of-the-hurricane focusing, simply bring your attention to an object and focus on it. This narrowing of your focus will help you eliminate outside distractions. You may want to focus on the ball or its sound, your strings, or even the sweat dripping from your brow. Once you are focused on your object of choice, you can then begin to expand your focus and take in everything around you. You will find this narrow-to-wide focusing to be very calming.

Regaining your focus is a challenge. Learning to adapt to the ever-changing dynamics on the court is empowering and a key to playing your best. All of the tools above can help you slow down, relax, and let go of adverse situations.

You Cannot Be Serious!

WORKOUT

Tools to Help You Regain Your Focus

The idea behind concentration is not necessarily to focus 100% of the time, but to know when you have lost your focus and regain it. Try the exercises below for five minutes each.

NO DISTRACTION EXERCISE:

Step #1:   With your eyes closed, notice your breath as you inhale and exhale.

Step #2:   As you inhale, visualize the number 1; as you exhale, silently say the number 1. Repeat this process.

Step #3:   If you get distracted or lose focus of the number 1, gently move on to the number 2 and visualize the number 2.

What number did you reach?_____

What did you do when you lost your concentration?

_____

_____

DISTRACTION EXERCISE:

Now, let's incorporate distractions. Turn on the TV, or have a friend try to distract you. Either way, close your eyes and follow the no-distraction protocol. Expect to lose your focus many more times.

What number did you reach?_____

How was this different?

_____

_____

Is it bad that you're losing your focus?

_____

The answer is no: What is important is understanding that you will lose your focus. What's key is bringing your focus back to what's important and what you can control at that time. It's impossible to focus 100% of the time. The top pros know how to relax and then focus at key times.

When you lose your focus, what are two things you can do to regain it?

1. _____

2. _____

Guess how many vibration dampeners are in the picture...
You cannot be serious! :)

Workout 22
Mental Point

Paradoxically, losing focus is not horrible. In fact, it is a natural occurrence; the key is being aware that you lost your focus and then changing it to bring yourself back to the present.

Match Point... Relax! But How?
Five Steps to Closing Out a Match

What the Pros Are Saying

I had my preparations in place. I knew I had nothing to lose and took my chances.

> — **Borna Coric**, *The Times of India: I am the best of my generation, says Borna Coric* by Susan Ninan, 1/4/15

I was losing those set points (in the tiebreak)… but I tried somehow to win the two points on my serve. It was 6-5 then. I thought, 'Go for it'. He managed to miss that shot after I played a few rallies back.

> — **Bernard Tomic**, *ausopen.com: Bernard Tomic times it right* by Matthew Trollope, 1/21/15

In the second set, I think when I realized that I finally can be in the finals, I got a little bit tense there. The game at 5-4 I was really like over thinking and couldn't really concentrate to be there in the moment. My serve wasn't working, and, yes, it was a little bit fighting with everything on the court at that moment.

> — **Lucie Safarova**, *rolandgarros.com: Safarova Through To First Grand Slam Final* by Matthew Trollope, 6/4/15

Key Principles

1. If it were easy, everybody would be doing it.
2. An opponent is most dangerous when they have nothing to lose.
3. Closing out a match is hard—expect that!

Match Point... Relax! But How?

How many times have you found yourself in a match in which you were just a few points or games from winning? Maybe the score was 6-3, 5-2, and you began to think, "Oh my gosh, this is great. I'm going to be the champion!" or, "Only four more points and the trophy's mine!" or even, "My friends are going to think I'm the greatest when I win." In another situation, you might be even closer to the "finish line." Maybe this time you are leading 6-2, 5-4 and serving in the crucial last game when you begin to think, "Just one more game!"

All weekend warriors, tournament and professional players have had these thoughts. The question becomes: How many of them have succumbed to such thoughts and went on to lose the match? The answer is, many! While it is true that many professionals and top-ranked players may lose their focus during critical times in a match, the truly mentally tough competitors become aware when this happens and are able to change and regain their focus immediately.

Paradoxically, losing focus is not horrible. In fact, it is a natural occurrence; the key is being aware that you lost your focus and then changing it to bring yourself back to the present. The problem is that when it's happening you may swear that you are concentrating. And you probably are—just on the wrong thing! Focusing on the events of the future immediately removes you from the present moment and takes you to a place where you have no control.

Furthermore, as your thoughts drift into the future, you lose touch with what's really important and what brought you to this point: playing without thinking, relying on your feel and natural instincts, and trusting your game—the game that got you to this moment in the first place.

When you lose focus, you usually begin to get tight physiologically: The blood flow gets diverted away from your hands and feet toward your deeper muscle groups, and your breathing becomes labored instead of deep and rhythmic. Next comes a loss of feel for your strokes: you are no longer focused on what you can control but instead you are worrying about your opponent, what others are going to say, and how you will explain away the loss. All of these physiological responses, combined with future-oriented thinking, cause your game to spiral farther out of control, particularly as you lose the next point and gasp for breath, grip the racket tighter, and try to find that elusive feel you had earlier.

So what can a player do? No doubt this is a difficult situation, but by employing the following five mental-toughness strategies—especially when you find your game spiraling out of control—you can give yourself the opportunity to get back on track and turn things around.

1. Become aware. The first step to combating loss of focus is to become aware that you have indeed lost it. When we talk about "concentration" in the sports arena, we are referring to the ability to focus on what's important and to let go of everything else. All players lose their focus at times; it's inevitable. The truly mentally-tough players, however, understand this. They don't beat themselves up when it happens and they immediately bring their focus back to what they can control. Remember Arthur Ashe in the 1975 Wimbledon final against Jimmy Connors at changeovers? That towel over his head served as a blanket that allowed him to center himself and bring his attention back to the present moment.

2. Refocus on the present. This is imperative, but how can you do it? First off, know that it takes a lot of courage and discipline to mentally refocus. However, what's the alternative? A free-fall! To refocus, bring your attention to your breath. Your breath is always completely present: just listen to it and its rhythm, sound, and feel as it enters and leaves your body. Or visualize yourself breathing relaxation in and breathing stress out, slowly letting go of the stressful air as you visualize it dissipating, as on a cold morning. Another present-moment awareness exercise is to breathe in through your nose to the count of three (if possible) and out through your mouth to the count of four. Or, make up your own pattern. These relaxing breathing patterns will help you to stay calm, relaxed, and mentally present during the most difficult transitional moments of a match. Other present-moment exercises to try include visualizing the feel of a shot, your rhythm, target zones, and shot patterns. These can all act as "anchors" to make you feel calm.

3. Change focus. Inevitably, athletes tend to lose focus when they think about the future, such as what might happen on the next point. The key here is to recognize this loss of focus and bring yourself back to the current point.

4. Let go of winning and of expectations. Remember, you cannot control whether you win or lose, or whether or not you hit a winner—your opponent has a say in that. Likewise, you cannot control the expectations others have of you. Paradoxically, the harder you try to close out the match point and win, the more physically tight you will become. Just play each point the best you can; if you do this, you will put yourself in the best position to win. If you don't win, you can walk away feeling positive about your effort.

5. Trust the process. Bring your attention to what you have to do to win the crucial point, which might include staying relaxed, returning the ball deep, or serving into your opponent's backhand. Ask yourself what it would feel like to hit a great serve. Your body knows; now is the time to trust it. Then ask yourself what it would feel like to play this point relaxed, and instinctively you will feel a release. In *The Inner Game of Tennis*, W. Timothy Gallwey talks about letting your body play the way it knows how to without interference from your (thinking) brain.

Using the strategies above will help you win the next point, game, or match. This is because they help you to begin the point in a calm and relaxed place. Remember, match point... relax! ...now you know how!

Match Point... Relax! But How?

WORKOUT

Try Softer, Not Harder

One of the biggest mental traps that athletes fall into is **"trying too hard." Fueled by frustration** or making the contest too important, trying too hard is usually a game of diminishing returns: The harder you try, the worse you'll do!

This is because **you put pressure on yourself,** rush yourself, and your **muscles tighten up.**

Peak performance always comes from being in a state of relaxed awareness, a place of letting go, where the actions happen without much conscious effort or thought.

When you become aware of **yourself trying too hard**, pressing, or rushing... **Shift your focus** of concentration away from the outcome or its importance to the present task at hand.

Remember you want to **relax and try "softer," not harder**.

What does the passage above make you aware of?

_____

_____

_____

How does this apply to your game?

_____

_____

_____

In order to try softer, not harder, what are three things you could do?

1. _____

2. _____

3. _____

Tennis Inside the Zone™

Workout 23
Mental Point

As a player, you are unable to directly control future points because you are unable to control your opponent. However, you can control whether you walk up to the line to serve or return serve on your terms in a focused and centered place.

The Towel is Your Friend:
How to Stay Calm Each Point

What the Pros Are Saying

I was maybe focusing on things I can't control, where I always know I need to focus on one point at a time, not worry about the score, result, things like that. So kind of getting out of the moment.

> — **Eugenie Bouchard**, *rolandgarros.com: An Interview With… Eugenie Bouchard,* 5/28/14

The key is to focus on one simple trigger to help let go of extraneous thoughts and regain the focus.

> — **Paul Annacone**, *Tennis Channel: J. Sock vs. Carrena Busta, 2nd Round French Open,* 5/28/15

Play inside the lines; don't let the distractions bother you. Keep your concentration.

> — **Pete Sampras**, *The Tennis Lovers Book of Wisdom*

Key Principles

1. Let go, relax, the point will still be there.
2. Use the towel to refresh and refocus.
3. Pros use the towel all the time... Do you?

The Towel is Your Friend

How many times have you seen the pros toweling off during a match? Often professional players towel off between every point. Some may walk towards the ball boy or ball girl to retrieve the towel, while others may make funny hand signals, simulating a windshield wiper going left to right, expecting the ball person to deliver the towel regardless of where they are on the court. Regardless of their idiosyncratic method, pros use the towel for much more than it appears.

When you're playing in a match, how often do you reach for your towel? In tight situations, do you take the time and walk over to your towel to give yourself a break from the action? Although the pros have the luxury of the towel being delivered to them anywhere on the court, you have to make a choice of where to place your towel. How many times do you find yourself on the deuce side and your towel is nestled in the corner on the ad side? Thoughts of "I can't take the time to go over there, it's going to take too much time," or "I wish the towel were on this side" run through your mind.

Next time, take the extra time to retrieve your sacred towel. It can be your best friend on the court. In addition to the fact that it mops off the perspiration on your face and arms, your towel is much more than you may have realized! It's a built-in break, a separation from the pressure of the match. No, it's not like going to your favorite ice cream shop or the beach, but it can provide you the necessary time you need to relax, bring your heart rate down, slow your breathing, and most importantly, decompress and get yourself centered for the next point. As a ritual, retrieving your towel breeds a familiarity that keeps you comfortable on the court and helps you stay in the present. It also can help you control the pace and rhythm of the match.

As a player, you are unable to directly control future points because you are unable to control your opponent. However, you can control whether you walk up to the line to serve or return serve on your terms in a focused and centered place.

So next time you play that long, physical point, take the time to retrieve your towel. Clear the sweat, and your mind, and take a break. Incorporate the towel into your between-point ritual. You might even consider placing a towel in the two corners on your side. That way you don't have to walk from the ad side to the deuce or vice versa. It's almost like you have your own personal ball person delivering your friend to you!

The Towel is Your Friend

WORKOUT

Most pros towel off between every point. Is it because they sweat more than non-pros? Hardly! They know what most junior players do not...

The towel is your friend. It can help you:

- slow things down
- catch your breath
- relax and get centered

- compose yourself
- let go of the previous point
- wipe sweat off your head and hands!

How about also attaching an index card to the corner of your towel? On the card can be a quote or phrase that motivates you, or a few things which you want to remember. They should be non-technical things which will provide you insight, help you relax, and motivate you. They should also be customized to the specific match, opponent, and circumstance.

For my index card, I usually write things like:

Match Play Card
- Look for my forehand
- Attack second serve
- Stay Patient
- Focus on what I can control
- Play like a tiger
- Compete like Rafal

What are your key points?

Match Play Card

Workout 24
Mental Point

The key to competing is adapting and adjusting to what is currently happening.

Competing in the Trenchs:
One Part Skill, Three Parts Will

What the Pros Are Saying

Nobody is unbeatable; the way he was playing we all thought he was not going to lose anytime soon. I tried not to think about his winning streak and his new ranking spot. I tried to focus on my game.

> — **Novak Djokovic**, *"In Semi Finals, Djokovic Shows That Nadal Can Be Beaten,"* by Josh Katzowitz, New York Times, Aug. 3, 2008

I don't know what my conversion rate was, but it was driving me insane. Every time I didn't take a break point it was like someone shot an arrow to me. I can't even explain how berserk I was going. At one point I said, 'Get me off the court'. Luckily I didn't. I was trying to tell myself when I was two sets to love down that I had a lot of chances in those two sets. Just keep pushing. I trust my game in the big moments when I need it. I kept hanging in there...

> — **Thanasi Kokkinakis**, *rolandgarros.com: Teenager Kokkinakis Downs Fellow Aussie Tomic* by Kate Battersby, 5/28/15

Key Principles

1. Play proud.
2. Your opponent is your partner, not the enemy.
3. Play within yourself, not without!

Competing in the Trenchs

It's 101 degrees, and the sun is beating down with no cloud cover in sight. The air is thick and moist, and the court surface is hot enough to fry an egg! The rubber on my soles is burning and my legs feel like live wires. As I look for cover, I see a sliver of shade behind the baseline in the corner by the fence. I've been out here for 3 hours and 20 minutes and the score is 4-6, 7-5, 6-all. The tiebreaker has just begun. I remember what my coach said: *"Tiebreakers are three parts will and one part skill."* At this point, I know it's all about how I compete. I'm thinking, "What do I have to do in the breaker?"

I reflect back and remember the hours of training I put in running, lifting weights, and conditioning myself for these moments. I also think of all the mental training I have practiced. Ugh, exhaustion is setting in. I wonder if I even have enough left. It's decision time. Either I push through and compete, or give in and fold. Another thought crosses my mind... why I am doing this in the first place? Yet I have made it my motto to compete to the fullest each and every point of each and every match. *I remind myself to bring my attention to my breath—it's so simple, but always seems to calm me and bring me into the present.*

This match has been a battle—the momentum has been like waves in the ocean, one after another, relentlessly crashing over each other. I still can't believe how my opponent played out of his mind in the first set. Okay, that's well beyond my control now. It's the third set tiebreaker! Every point is important. I remember my coach saying, *"The key to ideal competing is adapting and adjusting to what is currently happening."*

I know a change in strategy is essential to pull out this breaker and the match. It's serve and volley time. Not my typical strategy, but given the situation it would be advantageous. If I can serve into his body, I'm confident I can jam him and get an easy volley to control the point. Usually my game consists of big strokes from the baseline. This is where I'm most comfortable. However, after three hours in the baking sun, this situation is not typical! I remember my coach saying, *"The ability to be aware of what is going on in a match and be willing to change strategy when necessary is what separates the top 1% of competitors from the other 99%."*

My body aches, my stomach hurts, but there is nothing I can do except try to hydrate and manage my energy for just a bit longer. I've battled for three hours, and understand that despite my best preparation, I cannot control the way this match has affected my body. My mental training coach says, *"There are many things that you can't control, such as: You can't control how your opponent plays or acts, or his family yelling obnoxiously from the sideline. You cannot control the sun that has just begun to peek out from behind the clouds, blinding you on every serve attempt. You cannot directly control the result of this match—you can only control yourself, the shots you choose, and how you handle your emotions."*

I'm feeling like a fragile warrior, pushing through all the potential distractions. Is this what Isner and Mahut felt like in their epic first-round Wimbledon match? *I remind myself to stay focused on what I can control in my match. My job is to get myself in a position in which I can enter the next point in a calm, centered place. I use my breath to help me stay in the present and relax.*

The score in the tie-breaker is now 2-3, and my opponent is serving. I need to change my strategy for the return points. It's time to change the pace with some slow heavy deep balls... If I can throw him off his rhythm, and get him frustrated, I will have an opportunity to win. My ego tells me to keep pounding the ball, to try to overpower him, as I know I'm capable. But I know I have to push this aside. I cannot worry what other people think about my game, which is just another uncontrollable. I must do what I think is best to win and put aside any other concerns.

Good news... my opponent is getting rattled. He is yelling, upset, throwing his racket. I try not to respond to his antics. I can't allow him to rattle me. *Nothing is gained from being a poor sport. I try to find a balance of how to be a good sport as well as how to be a good competitor. The concepts are different, yet integrated. In order to compete at your best you have to respect the game and your opponent. This mindset keeps me in a focused, centered place.*

The tiebreaker score is now 7-6 in my favor. As I'm pushed back in a baseline rally and notice my opponent closing on the net, I manage to throw up a perfectly placed topspin lob over his outstretched backhand side—the tiebreaker is mine! The match is mine. We meet at the net and embrace.

This win was not easy; it ultimately wasn't about skill, but about competing in the moment. I had to adapt and adjust to the match momentum, focus on what I could control, and let go of what I could not. I had to battle without expectations, be willing to put my ego aside, and through it all I had to stay alert. These are the skills necessary to compete at your highest level. These are the tools used in mastering the science of competeology.

Competing in the Trenchs

WORKOUT

Pre-Match Intangibles Scale

This exercise will help you rate, become aware, and better understand key intangible factors prior to a match against a rival. Rate yourself and your opponent on each of these measurements (scale: 0 = not at all; 10 = very much). If you're unable to rate your opponent, complete the exercise only rating yourself.

Opponent:_____

Tournament:_____

Date:_____

	Myself	Opponent
Confidence:		
Momentum coming into the match		
Experience factor		
Physical readiness		
Mental readiness		
Hunger factor		
Concentration:		
Ability to focus on controllables		
Ability to manage uncomfortable situations		
Ability to make opponent uncomfortable		
Ability to stay emotionally balanced, and refocus		
Awareness		
Compete:		
Ability to stay the course (resilience, tenacity)		
Ability to bounce back from adversity/obstacles/setbacks (perseverance)		
Ability to adapt/adjust, switch plans (flexibility)		
Ability to make high-percentage choices		
Ability to play within self, take what opponent is giving you (patience)		

What does analyzing the Intangibles Scale make you aware of?

_____

_____

_____

What are you aware of in relation to your opponent?

_____

_____

_____

From the above, what are three things that would help you as you prepare for the match?

1. _____

2. _____

3. _____

How strong is your mental game?
Get iTZ! (Inside the Zone)

Workout 25
Mental Point

Success can only be achieved if
a player can proactively ride out
the wave and stay above water.
The goal is to simply stay afloat—
nothing fancy, just keep grinding.
Just as the calm existed before the
wave, the calm will resume after
the wave has passed. The question
becomes: is the player still afloat,
or have they let that wave throw
them off?

Riding the Waves:
Using Momentum to Win in Competition

What the Pros Are Saying

Eventually, after a disappointment, I could see these times not as losses, but as chances to evaluate what went wrong and figure out my strengths and weaknesses so that I could be that much better the next time.

> — **Billie Jean King**, *Pressure is a Privilege*

I think I'm on the right track. I started the year off a little slow. My results this year haven't been fantastic, but I feel like I have improved. I know I have.

> — **John Isner**, *Miami Herald: John Isner celebrates win by watching other tall athletes in NCAA tournament* by Michelle Kaufman and Bill Van Smith, 3/28/15

He was starting to play better at the end of the second set and the start of the third but over the course of a two or three-hour match there are going to be ups and downs. You just need to hit the reset buttons as quickly as possible so it doesn't last for two or three games.

> — **Andy Murray**, *The Guardian: Andy Murray against Jo-Wilfried Tsonga could decide US Open outcome* by Kevin Mitchell, 8/31/14

Key Principles
1. Sometimes it's about three parts will and one part skill.
2. Tennis is like a roller coaster: Many highs, many lows... just hang on.
3. It's not how you start, but how you finish.

Riding the Waves

A surfer sits out in the open ocean. The water is calm, the surfer is in complete control. Atop his surfboard, the surfer can enjoy the tranquility of his sport. However, he has not come out to the open water to enjoy tranquility. The surfer has ventured out in search of the big wave—the wave that will get his adrenaline pumping; the wave that will satisfy his craving for the thrill of competition; the wave that will push him to the absolute limit. He has come not for relaxation, but to embrace a challenge. The surfer looks forward to the biggest wave that may come his way. When the "big one" comes along it will undoubtedly test his physical abilities, challenge his mental game, and for a moment leave the surfer wondering if he can come out of the wave unscathed. But if he does, if he stays on the board and is able to ride the wave out, he will be ready for whatever comes up next. If he cannot stay on the board, he will spiral out of control, be thrashed under the water, and have no ability to take advantage of calm seas or handle a new wave.

There are parallels between this anecdote and a tennis player competing in a match. Just like the surfer, a tennis player may begin a match in complete control. They make the shots they are supposed to make, and win the points they are supposed to win. But then, just as a wave is bound to occur in the open ocean, a change and momentum shift is bound to occur in a tennis match. This is the natural evolution of nature and sports. Consistency plays a small role in both. The wave is impossible to stop—the momentum cannot be controlled. The best strategy is to continue to battle and try to ride it out.

A surfer may see a wave approaching far in the distance, just as a tennis player senses a change in momentum before it shows on the scoreboard. The wave may show itself either as a let down in one's own game, i.e. unforced errors, double faults, etc.; or as a boost in your opponent's game, i.e. aces, running winners, treeing, etc. Factors beyond the player's control, such as poor line calls or distracting fan conduct, can also lead to a momentum swing. These situations are inevitable in a match. But given the players' level of awareness of the specifics in a match, and their ability to sense the upcoming waves of momentum, players have the opportunity to mentally hunker down and prepare themselves for the impending change. There are times when the waves may be so sudden that all the player can do is hang on, grind it out, and hope to stay afloat.

Metaphorically, the wave is a change of momentum, often out of the player's control. Your opponent may hit a winner that paints the line, or hit a ball that hits the net and trickles over for a winner. The only hope to get through the wave is to ride it out. The wave should not be viewed as a setback or even an obstacle, but rather as an opportunity. An opportunity to test one's ability to remain focused, level-headed and in control. An opportunity to adapt and adjust one's game to what works best in changing situations. And an opportunity to push oneself both mentally and physically towards eventual success.

But success can only be achieved if a player can proactively ride out the wave and stay above water. The goal is simply to stay afloat—nothing fancy, just keep grinding. Countless times Rafael Nadal has demonstrated his ability to do this by saving break point after break point in a match. Just as the calm existed before the wave, the calm will resume after the wave has passed. The question becomes: is the player still on the board, or have they let that wave throw them off? If they are on the board, they are in a position to battle once the wave and momentum passes. However, if the player feels sorry for themselves, cannot stop thinking about past points, and is despondent about the negative turn of events, they will be completely unaware that the wave has passed. They will continue to spiral out of control. The player will not be able to take advantage of the newly found calm after the storm.

A player must recognize that momentum shifts are unavoidable in competition. It is just part of the rhythm of a match. Just as waves in the ocean ebb and flow, the course of a match constantly changes as well. This is a natural phenomenon, and the reason why we find sports so entertaining. Waves, momentum shifts, and adversity in a match should be seen as a challenge, something to be embraced. Perhaps Billie Jean King said it best when she texted Maria Sharapova "pressure is a privilege" before Sharapova beat Serena Williams in the 2004 Wimbledon final.

In the end, riding the big wave is the ultimate thrill. A surfer may struggle with the wave but stay on the board and ride the big wave out. Or they may completely fall off the board and capsize. When the surfer stays calm under pressure, they can persevere no matter how big and how many waves come their way. Once the surfer knows he can handle the waves, he can embrace even bigger waves, and hope for even bigger challenges. Only through challenging oneself, and confronting increasingly bigger obstacles can you improve. No one's saying the wave will be easy to ride out. The object is to battle it and stay afloat. Only by embracing the challenge of a big wave and testing one's limits will true potential be uncovered. Remember, nothing great is ever achieved without overcoming adversity.

Riding the Waves

WORKOUT

Hello–Goodbye Exercise

Pretend you are playing a match. Each game will be an opportunity for you to embrace something (say hello), and an opportunity to let go of something (say goodbye). For example, say hello to the nervousness of people watching and say goodbye to the fear of being judged.

Now, as you imagine playing the set, continue to fill in the blanks.

Set 1

Game 1 Hello: *nervousness of people watching*   Goodbye: *fear of being judged*

Game 2 Hello:_____ Goodbye :_____

Game 3 Hello:_____ Goodbye :_____

Game 4 Hello:_____ Goodbye :_____

Game 5 Hello:_____ Goodbye :_____

Game 6 Hello:_____ Goodbye :_____

Game 7 Hello:_____ Goodbye :_____

Game 8 Hello:_____ Goodbye :_____

Game 9 Hello:_____ Goodbye :_____

Game 10 Hello:_____ Goodbye :_____

Game 11 Hello:_____ Goodbye :_____

Game 12 Hello:_____ Goodbye :_____

Tiebreaker Hello:_____ Goodbye :_____

Set Score Hello:_____ Goodbye :_____

Match Hello:_____ Goodbye :_____

 Workout 26
Mental Point

Matches are not the time to analyze technique—it is the opportunity to simply play, by getting "out of your mind" and allowing the body to do what it has been trained to do.

Get Outta Your Mind:
It's the Only Way to Compete!

What the Pros Are Saying

Obviously I was not going to leave the French Open without having tried everything out there. So it was tough. Would have loved to have won the breaker, would have loved to come back in the first set, but wasn't so… I'm already thinking what I'm going to do the next few days, because Wimbledon is going to be a big goal for the season.

> — **Roger Federer**, *NY Times*

It doesn't really feel real at the moment. I didn't feel as if I was playing out there, it almost felt as if I was just watching.

> — **Nick Kyrgios**, *Tennis-X blog: Beating Federer Is A Bigger Win For Me Than Beating Nadal At Wimbledon* by Tom Gainey, 5/6/15

Then I tried to play more relaxed… I remember, because I connected to another level that I didn't know existed. I start to play in another dimension.

> — **Gustavo Kuerten**, *rolandgarros.com: Guga returns to Roland-Garros* by Matt Trollope, 5/30/15

Key Principles
1. Remember your training; trust your instincts.
2. Overthinking leads to paralysis.
3. Listen carefully—your body knows what to do.

Get Outta Your Mind

We have all heard people say, "She played out of her mind!" referring to someone who played exceptionally well and beyond expectations. As an athlete, have you ever performed out of your mind? Either pitching to perfection, running like the wind, or serving lights out? Maybe there is more to this "out of your mind" concept than meets the eye. The idea is ultimately a metaphor for playing within yourself, where everything is effortless, where little thought occurs, and optimal performance just happens. In this workout, I will discuss how literally getting "out of your mind" is the best way to reach optimal personal peak performance in competitive sports.

When an athlete plays "in their mind" they are not playing from instinct. They are usually over-analyzing, and their thoughts are cluttered and disorganized. These thoughts interfere with their ability to play. Further, their thoughts are in the past and future, tied to expectations, ego, excitement, and fears. Essentially, their thoughts are weighing them down— athletes describe it as playing with an imaginary weight around their waist and trying to run, jump, hit, and concentrate while their mind is over-thinking every move.

We all know what happens when this kind of mentality creeps in—the dreaded spiral where a player loses control! Physically and mentally it looks like this: An initial loss of focus, fear about what might be or what is occurring, tightened muscles, heavy breathing, and loss of feeling. Then the poor play follows, usually ending in disappointment and defeat. The only way to optimize performance is to play in the moment (present), and to respond to situations with calm awareness as opposed to reacting out of ego, fear and anxiety. I call this the "eye of the hurricane," calm on the inside yet aware and active on the outside.

The key to staying in the moment is within all of us—the secret lies in our bodies. Our body is always in the present moment. When an athlete becomes aware of his or her body, such as the rhythm in their hips when they swing a racket, they simplify things and enter a place of curiosity where they are simply noticing their present actions. This moves them away from distracting ego, fear, and anxiety-driven thoughts. In fact all of the "what-if," "shoulda," or "coulda" thoughts are no longer in the way, because the focus is on observation rather than judgment. Essentially, by getting "out of your mind," you get "out of your way" and simply allow the technique you have practiced and your performance to happen or flow in the present. If an adjustment is necessary, it can then be made without judgment.

How can a player shift their focus "outta their mind" (thoughts, past, future, and judgments) and into their body (present)? It starts with a keen awareness; when they become aware of being submerged in over-thinking, fear or that recognizable negative spiral, the idea is to simplify things and shift attention to something in the present. For example, the athlete may focus on their breathing, or a place in the body they feel calm and centered. This refocus "out of your mind" and into your body serves as a reconnection to the present—a place of calm and observation. From this place the athlete can play by observing and noticing instead of judging their technique or performance.

Ultimately, by the start of the match, game, or performance, the athlete has the skills necessary to compete at their personal highest level. The competition is not the time to analyze technique—it is the opportunity to simply play, by getting "out of your mind" and allowing the body to do what it has been trained to do. It is easy to let your mind creep toward the result, get caught up in expectations, question whether others are judging your performance, or think about the missed opportunity of a previous exchange. Yet the aforementioned tools can help the player to keep his or her attention out of the mind and in the present, able to respond to the moment.

Athletes love those times when they feel immersed in the competition, competing with great effort for sustained periods of time, and ultimately playing inside the zone. Shawn Green, in his book The Way of Baseball, talks about how he used the batting tee and focus on his breathing to get out of his mind and re-connect with his natural swing. Billie Jean King, in her book *Pressure is a Privilege*, also talks about how she uses her breath to limit distraction and stay inside the zone. So next competition, shift your focus "outta your mind" away from fears or judgments and "inside the zone" to your breath and body, and begin the path to unlocking your potential.

Get Outta Your Mind

WORKOUT

The Frog and the Centipede

A frog was sitting on a patch of grass by his pond one sunny morning
when a large centipede passed by.
The frog watched this creature with fascination, then
said, "Excuse me, can I ask you a question?"
"Why, yes, of course," replied the centipede, pausing in his stride.
"I am amazed at the way you can proceed so harmoniously
with your one hundred legs," said the frog. "Can you explain
to me how you manage to keep them in order?"
The centipede reflected for a moment. "You know, I have never really
thought about it," he said. "Let me see if I can demonstrate it for you."
And he started to walk, thinking about which leg should follow another.
Immediately, he fell down and had great difficulty getting up again.
"You are dangerous!" he said to the frog angrily.
"Never again ask such questions!"

After reading this poem, what does it make you aware of?

_____

_____

How does this relate to your game?

_____

_____

List three ways this insight will help your game:

1. _____

2. _____

3. _____

Great Mural as you enter the Harlem Tennis
Center in NYC.

Omega Workshop: Scrapbook Memory

During family week, each year, I run a workshop called "Unleash the Player Within". The workshop focuses on the mental game of tennis and helping them to play INSIDE THE ZONE!

Standing alongside the Omega courts which have been dedicated to my friend and mentor Dr. Jena Marcovicci. This is the Dance of Tennis Plaque in memory of Jena.

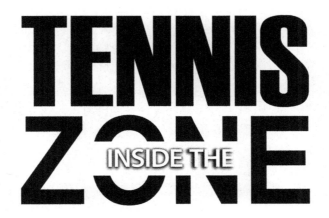

Section 4
POST-MATCH WORKOUTS

Post-Match Workouts

It's All Practice

Martial artists understand that competition brings with it a separate set of challenges, therefore whether they win or lose, they see it as practice and part of the journey.

Martial artists understand success is reached along the journey, not at the destination. They see the competition as something to learn and grow from. Further obstacles, failures and successes are to be expected and necessary experiences in striving for a goal.

What would happen if you approached tournaments the same way martial artists approach competition?

— Rob Polishook, M.A., C.P.C.

Workout 27
Mental Point

How do you cope with the disappointment? How do you bounce back from a painful defeat? First off, let's acknowledge, it's not easy and it hurts!

Losing Stinks!
Five Steps to Dealing With a Tough Loss

What the Pros Are Saying

I really do love this game, especially after last week when I must have said that night a thousand times, I hate tennis more than anything in life.

> — **Mirjana Lucic-Baroni**, *NY Times: Simona Halep Falls as Other Top Players Cruise at French Open* by Ben Rothenberg, 5/27/15

I had expectations for myself… that's to me the biggest disappointment, the negative part of it, of course. Of course I shed a few tears, but it should hurt. It should hurt. And it does hurt.

> — **Grigor Dimitrov**, *Bleacher Report: How Grigor Dimitrov is Developing into the Next Tennis Superstar* by Jeremy Eckstein, 2/7/14

The Chinese word for crisis carries two elements of meaning: they are danger and opportunity. No matter what the difficulty of the circumstances, how bad things may look, feel and seem. At the heart of every crisis lies a tremendous opportunity. Great things lie ahead for the one who knows the secret to finding opportunity within each crisis.

> — Chinese Arts Poster

Key Principles
1. The only time you lose is when you give up.
2. Losing offers a fresh start.
3. Failure is feedback and part of the process.

Losing Stinks!

Imagine this: You're playing in front of 200 spectators, grinding it out on the hard courts under the hot sun. The first set you've won 7-5. Then in a tight second set you narrowly lose 6-7 and that was after holding two match points! You're now in the third set tie-breaker and the score is 5-6. Your opponent hits a let court, trickling over the net. You hear an echo in your head... game, set, match. It's another disappointing loss! 7-5, 6-7, 6-7. But this one hurts even more as you had two match points in the second set and opportunities to break in the third. Slowly you walk up to the net and shake your opponent's hand. Your hand feels limp and your body feels like the energy has been sucked out by a vacuum cleaner. Your legs are wobbly and your eyes are glazed over. You simply can't believe what has happened.

So what's a player to do? How can you get over this disappointment? Your parents and friends tell you it's nothing, just move on. You'll do better next time, they say. Don't you just hate that phrase?! However, still covered in sweat and feeling partially paralyzed, you hear them but can barely say anything. You feel as if you have lockjaw, unable to mutter a word. In your mind you are still replaying the points that you feel you should have won, holding on to the advantages for dear life.

So let me repeat... what's a player to do? How do you cope with the disappointment? How do you bounce back from a painful defeat? First off, let's acknowledge: It's not easy and it hurts! However, at some point, when the pain starts lessening, anywhere from a few hours to a day or so, it becomes imperative to view the match through another lens. That is, how do you begin to pick the pieces up? And what must you do next time to get better? How will you take advantage of certain situations and continually put yourself in a position to get over the hump?

The following are five steps to help you, the broken player, experience and move past a disappointing performance. Equally so, this list is great for parents, coaches, and friends as they try to support the player during the process of disappointment, release, and rebounding.

1. A right to be disappointed: You've earned the right to be disappointed. Let's face it: after putting it all on the line, competing with all your heart, it is practically impossible to put on a smiling face and just forget things after a close loss. Give yourself some time. It's okay to be disappointed. In fact, it's even expected. Why wouldn't you be? You care, you practiced, you're a warrior, and you fought like one! Disappointment is a natural emotion—it even hurts, and that's okay too. It's not something that needs to be fixed. It is time that usually heals it. Disappointment can be equated to mourning a loss. Allow yourself the time to decompress, feel your feelings, and settle down. Paradoxically, by allowing yourself to experience the disappointment you also allow yourself the opportunity to release and resolve the painful feelings. One of the things that makes victory so sweet, and motivates us so, is knowing the feeling and experience of disappointment.

2. One step closer: Believe it or not, you are actually one step closer to your goals! The great Babe Ruth used to say every time he struck out, "I'm one step closer to hitting a home run!" Babe would learn from being up at bat, and change his strategies every time he stepped up to the plate. You can do the same. It took Rafael Nadal many years to gain the number one ranking. Each time he lost during this period, he wondered how he could improve and do better the next time. It's obvious he learned a lot after beating Roger Federer on grass and hard courts. Don't forget, slumps fit in here too. It may look like you're going nowhere, or even backwards, but keep on plugging away and learning. Maybe the competition is getting stronger or the match-up is not as favorable. Remember the saying: It's always darkest before the dawn. In other words, the sun rises after the darkest hour! That slump may be a major learning curve that just needs to be ridden out, much like a wave. And just beyond the wave is smooth sailing. Hang on...

3. Failure provides feedback: If you listen you become aware. Failures, setbacks and obstacles always throw us for a loop, but it's the true champion who can readjust and glean valuable feedback. Feedback should be viewed without judgment and as a learning opportunity in which you can make changes and adapt, adjusting to the situation next time. Think about it: Was there ever a great champion, individual, or team that didn't learn from failures, setbacks and obstacles? All great champions know why they are competing and use this "Big Why" to get themselves back on track. How long did fans judge Federer during his early days? They said he was all hype. Federer was simply taking names and learning along the way. Soon enough he flourished and, as of the printing of this book, he has 17 Grand Slam titles. He used failure as feedback en route to his rise and now, as we watch, he has regained the #1 ranking.

4. Reframe it! Simply stated, after you have decompressed ask yourself the basic questions. What's another way to look at this loss or situation? How can I find something positive from it? What's the lesson here? Even though you lost, what can you learn? And don't forget: Give yourself some credit for showing up and putting yourself on the line. How many others are competing with such a heart as yours?

5. Focus on the process, not the outcome. This is probably one of the most important points and the major one that all other points can probably be folded into. While you lost this performance, it is another step toward your ultimate goal. The match gave you valuable experience and exposed you to the situational pressure of match play. This is highly valuable and can't be duplicated in practice. Remember, all great champions have to pay their dues.

Losing Stinks!

WORKOUT

It's not how hard you can hit that matters, it's how hard you can get hit, and keep bouncing back—that's what life (sports) is about.

— Sylvester Stallone, Rocky

First off... let's acknowledge that it hurts to lose, especially when you have put yourself on the line and tried your best in that specific situation and time. Second, let's acknowledge that it's hard to bounce back from a painful loss but you can do it!

What was a time you experienced a difficult loss? Describe it:

_____

_____

_____

What are three things you learned from the loss?

1. _____

2. _____

3. _____

How can you use these lessons in future matches?

_____

_____

_____

If you did, what would happen?

_____

_____

_____

 Workout 28
Mental Point

You don't have to like failure, in fact you can even hate it! However, you must recognize it is necessary for success. You deserve to be disappointed and even angry after a setback; however, this does not have to be a permanent state.

Mistakes, Setbacks and Failure:
The Only Way to Win

What the Pros Are Saying

I get very pissed off and disappointed. It's a process, and all I'm asking is… I can be hard on myself. But I'm getting better every day. And I believe if I do so, I will eventually get to where I want to be. So I have to be patient.

> — **Milos Raonic**, *Men's Journal: Is Milos Raonic the Future of Tennis?* by Kevin Gray, 2014

The greatest glory in living lies not in never falling, but in rising every time we fall.
> — **Nelson Mandela**

Ever tried. Ever failed. No matter. Try again. Fail again. Fail Better.
> — Tattoo on Stan Wawrinka's left arm, quote from writings of **Samuel Beckett**.

Key Principles
1. Failure is feedback.
2. It's not how hard you can hit, but how hard you can get hit and bounce back.
3. It's not whether you make mistakes, but how you rebound.

Mistakes, Setbacks and Failure

No one likes to make mistakes in practice, nobody likes to encounter setbacks and obstacles in games, and certainly no one likes to fail and lose in a tournament. It's hurtful, disappointing, frustrating, and sometimes feels like you are back to square one! But there is a secret—a secret that only the top players know. Many top juniors fail to grasp what players such as Roger Federer, Rafael Nadal, Andy Murray and others have realized and used to their advantage as they have developed into the best the game has to offer. This knowledge is that mistakes, setbacks, obstacles and failure are inevitable. Further, it is how a player learns and adapts from these difficult experiences that determines whether their potential is fulfilled.

Sure, top players are disappointed by mistakes, setbacks, obstacles and losing—in fact they hate it more than anyone. However, they also realize it is an inevitable part of their process, and they don't allow disappointments to sidetrack them when striving towards their ultimate goal: continuous improvement and long-term success.

Case in point: The 2008 Los Angeles Lakers were overwhelmed in six games in the NBA finals by the Boston Celtics. With essentially the same roster, the team used that experience as motivation to win the title in 2009, and did so in impressive fashion. This team learned from their experiences, changing their strategy to continually improve. Success is like climbing a mountain—there is no such thing as a straight path. The player and team has to continually adjust and navigate switchbacks, pause at certain points, and even go backwards in order to find a path which can take them higher.

I like to share an example of a player who was known as a consummate hot-head in the juniors. He began his professional career ranked #803. In year one he had two wins and three losses. In his second year, he lost in the first round of every outdoor tournament he entered, was 0-2 in the Davis Cup, did not reach the main draw in two Grand Slam tournaments, and ended the year with 12 wins and 14 losses. The third year he lost in the first round of 21 out of 38 ATP tournaments, and ended the year with 30 wins and 27 losses. After sharing this background, I once asked a group of juniors what they would do if they were this player. Most raised their hands and explained that they would quit and find another job. Fortunately, Roger Federer had other plans!

This brings to mind a phrase I often use: "Failure is feedback." This phrase refers to the idea that failure provides a valuable window for the athlete, in which they can use the feedback from a negative experience to make necessary adjustments and changes in their game. These changes will quickly get them back on the proper path towards their goals. However, without awareness of a player's own weaknesses, the player will continue to do the same things, make the same mistakes time after time, and spiral downward.

Another famous phrase is, "Failure is breakfast for champions." This refers to the fact that in order to learn, an athlete needs to fail enough to learn better methods. They need to risk, experiment, and be curious. Of course failure will sometimes come along with such experimentation, but so will success! Think about a skier or a surfer: If they don't fall, chances are the slopes and waves are not challenging enough. In fact, skiers and surfers are always looking for the next great challenge and thrill. They are never satisfied to repeat the same run, instead looking for a steeper hill or more massive wave. James Blake had this to say in his best-selling book Breaking Back: "*My greatest professional successes occurred after I had faced my most personal challenges. I used to think this was ironic; now I realize that success flows directly from having cleared those hurdles.*"

You don't have to like failure, in fact you can even hate it! However, you must recognize it is necessary for success. You deserve to be disappointed and even angry after a setback. However, this does not have to be a permanent state. Rather, by utilizing a heightened awareness of what happened, you can begin to work through the things that may have gone wrong. You may have played poorly today, but that doesn't mean you will play poorly every day. Your future results are not set in stone. If you lost, that doesn't mean you are a loser, but you simply lost today; tomorrow is another day with another opponent. Additionally, it's vital to understand that your main opponent is yourself, and that the competition is there to help you gauge your progress and improve. Lastly, understanding that you are a work in progress and not a fixed entity opens the door for improvement, change, and different results.

The key point here is that winning is a process that is littered with setbacks, mistakes, obstacles, and failures. If processed correctly, an athlete will recognize these setbacks as temporary. They can learn from them and ultimately move forward towards their goal. Albert Einstein says the definition of insanity is doing the same thing time after time, yet expecting different results! They say Edison successfully discovered 8,000 ways *not* to make a light bulb. Abraham Lincoln didn't win an election until the presidential race! These great American heroes certainly used mistakes, setbacks, and failure as feedback. How will you? The next time you lose, ask yourself: What can I learn from this? How can I use this experience to make an adjustment in strategy or technique to reach my ultimate goal? Remember, behind every crisis lies a far more valuable opportunity.

Mistakes, Setbacks and Failure

WORKOUT

No one has ever achieved something great without encountering adversity. Mistakes are the portals to discovery.

— James Joyce

A mistake, setback or loss is never the problem. The problem lies when we don't step back to learn from our mistakes. Mistakes provide feedback. The only mistake is not learning from it.

Next time you make a mistake, try not to judge it or yourself. Be aware of what happened and let it go. Trust yourself to make an adjustment the next time you're in the same situation.

List three mistakes you made in the last match you played:

1. _____

2. _____

3. _____

Choose one, and describe how you judged yourself at the time.

_____

_____

_____

_____

What do you notice when you talk to yourself this way?

_____

_____

_____

_____

What could you say to yourself after a mistake that would be helpful?

_____

_____

_____

_____

_____

_____

_____

_____

Create a Mistake Ritual. What short routine could you do to help yourself let go of mistakes? Describe it.

_____

_____

_____

_____

_____

_____

_____

_____

_____

_____

_____

_____

_____

 Workout 29
Mental Point

It's important to remember you must focus on the present, compete, and let go of uncontrollable expectations. Just play proud!

I'm Better! How Could I Lose!
The 7 Biggest Mistakes the Favorites Makes

What the Pros Are Saying

Part of me was already thinking about possibly holding the trophy, you know. So this time, I really tried to change that and don't think about that at all and just focus on my game. There were some moments where this thought would still come up, but I managed to control [accept] it much better.

> — **Ana Ivanovic**, *"Ivanovic, the New No. 1, is Also Tops in Paris,"* by Christopher Clarey, *New York Times*, Jun. 8, 2008

Entering a tournament like this, you know how to prepare. You go into a first round match like today in a calm matter, without any panic, whereas maybe ten years ago or more, you are so worried about everything, you hope you are going to play okay…

> — **Roger Federer**, *Tennis Channel interview after 1st round win against Alejandro Falla, 5/24/15*

It started last year because I was so hyped on getting to 18 and I lost every Grand Slam early. I didn't make it to any quarterfinals. Then after Wimbledon I decided to just not necessarily not care, but just relax.

> — **Serena Williams**, *ausopen.com: Serena Embraces the Challenge* by Alexandra Willis, 1/29/15

Key Principles

1. Winning isn't just about technique, it's about how you compete.
2. Perfection is rarely required to win.
3. Let go of expectations: They can't be controlled.

I'm Better! How Could I Lose!

"'m the better player, how did I lose?" Does this phrase sound familiar? Imagine this: It was the finals of the annual 16-and-under tournament, the weather was hot and muggy, and the sun was beaming down like a laser. The time was 3 p.m. and the stands were jammed with fans, coaches, and local media. The match featured the heavily-favored local boy, Sander Myles, and his opponent, Paul Robinson. They had never met before, but many people suspected that Myles was the stronger player based on his reputation and ranking. Some people even referred to Robinson as a pusher. Robinson referred to himself as a competitor.

The match did not go as most expected. Myles, who had looked so self-assured during the warm-up, seemed surprised by the steady Robinson. At some point in the match Myles got a bit deflated, began missing some easy balls, berated himself a few times, and soon was shaking hands at the net with his head down. The score was 4-6, 2-6. The boy now looked shell-shocked. He had no idea how he could lose to a fellow with strokes like that. But one thing he did know was that Robinson never gave up, always ran down that last ball that seemed out of reach, and maintained a steady level of play until the last point.

All club, high school and tournament players have probably experienced this situation at least once in their competitive career. Yet how many of these players really seek to understand what happened, and try to put a plan together so that history doesn't repeat itself in the next match?

This workout is intended to highlight the biggest *mistakes* a favorite can make against a supposed underdog.

1. Overconfidence: How many players have you seen begin a match feeling like they are entitled to win based on seeding, technique, or past results? The downfall with such a mindset is that focusing on off-court factors will take a player out of the present moment, and distract them from performing their best during the match.

2. Focus on winning: We all want to win! However, it's important to remember that winning is not 100% in our control; we must also take into account that we have an opponent who also wants to win. Whenever a player begins to think ahead to the result, he or she should change their focus away from the outcome and back to the process of the present moment—on something they can control. They could ask themselves, "What do I need to do to play this point well?" It might start with focusing on their breath and getting themselves in a centered and relaxed place. (See Workout 11, "How to Play in the Moment: It's as Easy as Breathing.")

3. Listen to the hype: Your friends, teammates, coaches, and maybe even the media are going to be singing your praises. While these accolades are nice to hear, they will not get you one point on the scoreboard. All your efforts should be on what you can do to prepare for the match. This mindset isn't glamorous, but if you listen to the true champions, this is how they approach each match. They focus only on what they can control, and let the rest go.

4. Rely on talent alone: Talent is great—it makes the sport easier to learn for some than for others. However, everyone eventually faces an opponent where talent alone isn't enough to earn the victory. In fact, sometimes talent is a curse for a player who views his or her ability as "enough" to get results. Talent, work ethic, on-court intelligence, and the will to *compete* are all crucial factors in player development.

5. Lack competitive intensity: If you ask anyone what percentage of a match is about competing, and what percentage is about playing your best, the answer is that competing is more important. It's extremely rare that someone is able to play their best all the time. However, a player can always control how they compete.

6. Lose composure: Sure, if you're the favorite, everybody is expecting you to win. Therefore when things get close, the underdog is inspired—while for you, the frustration kicks in. Before you know it, the negative self-talk starts, the racket flies, and suddenly you have lost control

on the court. The favorite always has to be prepared to give their best effort, remain focused, and work for every point no matter what the level of player they are competing against.

7. Awareness: Oftentimes the favorite is not even aware of what's happening on the court with regard to tactics and strategy. This is particularly the case because they have a preconceived notion of how the match should play out. Once again, their focus is on the past or future and they are playing to an ideal instead of playing in the present. It's important to play the match without expectations except that you will compete fully and attempt to play your best. This open mindset will allow the player to see what's unfolding before them, and to make the necessary adjustments.

As a favorite, it's important to remember you must focus on the present, compete, and let go of uncontrollable expectations. The infamous Tiki Barber, former football player for the New York Giants, was once asked what his mother said to him before games. Tiki replied that regardless of whether he was the favorite or the underdog, "She told me to *play proud*." These words are simple, empowering, and show respect to the person, opponent, and game—a perfect mindset for entering any match.

I'm Better! How Could I Lose!

WORKOUT

When an athlete focuses on what they cannot control, stress goes up, breathing increases, muscles tighten, confidence falls, performance lowers and slumps continue... this is because you have no direct control over these things. They change from moment to moment.

When an athlete focuses on what they can control, they will be more positive, relaxed, and open to opportunities. This is because the process is within their control.

Peak performance demands that an athlete focus on what they can control.

<u>List controllables and uncontrollables for your next match.</u>

CONTROLLABLES	UNCONTROLLABLES
preparation	*weather (sun/wind/rain)*

What does completing the above table make you aware of?

_____

_____

_____

How can you use it to help you?

_____

_____

What are the main three uncontrollables that that you lose your focus on?

1. _____

2. _____

3. _____

What happens when you lose your focus?

_____

_____

When you lose your concentration, what controllables could you re-focus on?

_____

_____

Imagine changing your focus to something on your list that you can control. How do you think that could help?

_____

_____

What would if take to make that concentration change?

_____

_____

Is it worth doing? _____

Workout 30
Mental Point

Whether a player wins or loses, they should always ask themselves some key questions about their performance. The goal of asking questions is to raise awareness of what happened, so you can analyze your performance and that of your opponent.

Sweet Victory!
Seven Questions to Ask After a Win (or Loss)

What the Pros Are Saying

If you can meet with Triumph and Disaster
And treat those two impostors just the same...
> — **Rudyard Kipling**, "If—" 1910 (displayed over the play-ers' entrance at Wimbledon Center Court)

One thing Venus always tells me: A win is a win, and as long as you live to survive the next day, you can always improve.
> — **Serena Williams**, *NY Times: Serena Williams Struggles, but Clears a Mental Hurdle at the French Open* by Ben Rothenberg, 5/28/15

I had many matches in three sets in last few weeks. I lost three of them very tough. And first moment when I left the court I said that I'm disappointed that I lost them, but now I'm thinking better and I feel that I was very close and that was important…I have learned many, many things from those matches.
> — **Simona Halep**, *rolandgarros.com: Halep: "Now I Know What To Do"* by Matt Trollope, 5/22/15

Key Principles

1. Little successes add up to big wins.
2. Win or lose, you can always learn from your performance.
3. The only loss is when you don't learn.

Sweet Victory!

Congratulations! You just won a grueling, hard-fought three-set match! You're drenched, tired, and in need of fluids. After you take care of the physical recuperation, it's time to think about the mental part. Specifically: What do you do now? How can you build on the success you had? Or even: What aspects of your game could you improve? Sometimes after winning a match, players get satisfied with the win and simply move on to the next match without evaluating their play. This is not the time to rest on your laurels, but to stay grounded, humble and continue to improve and build on what's working and analyze what's not working.

Many coaches like to say that you learn more from your losses than from your wins. Certainly, this can be true. Oftentimes they stand out and hurt more, which in turn forces you to understand where things did not go according to plan. However, don't be fooled: There is important information to be gained from both a loss and a win. Remember that winning or losing is out of your control. Because of this, the smart player goes beyond the results and looks to improve no matter the outcome.

Whether a player wins or loses, they should always ask themselves some key questions about their performance. The goal of asking questions is to raise awareness of what happened, analyzing your performance and that of your opponent. By taking ten minutes to do this (see the Workout), a player sets him- or herself up to understand what needs to stay the same and what

needs to change in their game.

The remainder of this workout will highlight seven key questions that players should ask themselves after a sweet win or a tough loss.

1. Briefly describe the score and conditions of the match. This is simply a question for the player to log the score and write down their overall impressions of the match. It might be as simple as, "I won 6-4, 5-7, 6-3. The courts were very fast with no shade cover. I played a good first set, and then dropped my intensity in the second set, but picked it up again in the third." This question is not to be judgmental, but simply to note the objective facts about the competition.

2. How did I feel mentally and physically coming into the competition? It's important to check in and understand how you felt in order to assess where you need to go. Oftentimes a player might be coming off another big win, or they may have played three matches in 24 hours and are mentally and physically tired, or they are coming off an injury, or they are returning to competition after a break. All these factors influence how you prepare and play, therefore they should be noted. Understanding these issues will help a player and coach be aware of the situation and make changes if necessary. Additionally, a player or coach can identify a tactic that is reaping positive results and reproduce it.

3. What are three things I did well? It's important to identify our strengths and winning shot patterns in competition so we can continue to use and build on them. This awareness will provide feedback to continue building on strengths. There is usually no such thing as a perfect performance, and there is also no such thing as a completely flawed performance. It is always somewhere in between. Certainly we all have our weaknesses—however, our job in competition is to create a situation where we put ourselves in a position to play the shots we want in the situations we want. If we can do this, we have the best chance to compete and, subsequently, win. Answers to this question might include: "I served well and immediately looked to take control of the point;" or, "I moved forward and was aggressive." Then ask yourself: How can I continue to build on these positives?

4. What are three things which I can improve on? Again, if you won? Congratulations. If you lost? Hang in there! There are always areas to further develop and improve. Look at Rafael Nadal: He entered the 2010 U.S. Open with a much-improved serve. It was revealed that he switched his grip a month before the competition. This is a perfect example of tweaking an already-successful game to make it better. Apply such wisdom to your own game by noting weaknesses and how to improve them. Then ask yourself: How can I implement these improvements in my next match?

5. If I played this opponent again, what would I do the same, and what would I do differently? This question will help you analyze the strategic aspects of the competition. Ira Miller, a well-respected colleague, told me that "Winning is about making your opponent uncomfortable" with regard to shot selection. A great example of this is when Nadal plays Roger Federer: Nadal always plays his big topspin forehand to Federer's one-handed backhand. This usually forces Federer back and puts Rafa on the offensive.

6. What are my next steps? Who can help me? This is an important question as it makes the player think about what they need to do next, and subsequently who could help them get to the next step. It might be a short-term answer to help them prepare for the next competition, or a longer-term one to help them prepare for the next level in their development.

7. How do I feel about my effort and play regarding the match? Again, this question is a check-in question. It's an opportunity for the player to simply identify where they are mentally and physically. An answer might be, "I'm exhausted, but feel good about my effort, and am confident going into the finals tomorrow."

In summary, a player who takes the time to answer these questions after a match will be more aware of where their game is mentally, tactically, strategically, and physically. Additionally, by documenting your matches and progress, the information will serve as a reference point towards your ongoing development as well as when you play the same player or a player with a similar game in future matches. Lastly, after a while, players and coaches will be able to see trends and patterns in which they can make necessary adjustments. Remember, if the result is a sweet victory... congratulations! If it's a tough loss... you can still bounce back!

Sweet Victory!

WORKOUT

Seven Questions to Ask After a Win (or Loss)

"The match doesn't end after the last point... that's actually the time to evaluate what happened, what you might do differently, and how you can improve next time."

— Rob Polishook

Date:_____

Singles	☐	Tournament	☐	Indoor	☐	Hard Court	☐
Doubles	☐	League Match	☐	Outdoor	☐	Har Tru/Clay	☐

Match location / weather:

_____

Opponent's name(s) & team:

_____

My partner's name:

_____

Won ☐   Lost ☐

Score:_____

Overall record vs. opponent:_____

1. Describe the match:

_____

_____

_____

_____

Tennis Inside the Zone™

2. How did I feel mentally and physically coming into the match?

_____

_____

_____

3. What are three things I did well?

- _____

- _____

- _____

4. What are three things I didn't do well which I can improve on?

- _____

- _____

- _____

5. If I played this opponent again, what would I do the same? What would I do differently?

_____

_____

_____

6. What are my next steps to making these adjustments? Who can help me?

_____

_____

_____

7. How did I feel about my effort and play regarding the match?

_____

_____

_____

 Workout 31
Mental Point

Anyone who has experienced an injury understands how the mental scars don't just disappear when the doctor says you're cleared to play.

Flight, Fight, Freeze:
The Seven Biggest Fears That Paralyze Athletes

What the Pros Are Saying

When I think I'm not playing great today… I think back to this guy (my brother) that doctors said was one day away from dying… So I think any struggle… I have on the court is very small compared to actual reality.

> — **Jack Sock**, *the Kansas City Star: After brother's near-death experience, Jack Sock is thankful for more than tennis* by Vahe Gregorian, 4/25/15

My nerves were getting the best of me. It happens to everybody. Anybody who says they don't choke, they're lying.

> — **Pete Sampras**, *You Can Quote Me on Than* by Paul Fein, 2001, p.47

You've got to get to that stage in your life where going for it is more important than winning or losing.

> — **Arthur Ashe**, *The Tennis Lover's Book of Wisdom* pg. 35

Key Principles

1. The athlete is a person first and a performer second.
2. Choking happens!
3. Our biggest fears usually come out when we feel most vulnerable.

Flight, Fight, Freeze

How many times have you heard the following from a coach, parent, or teammate: "If only he played to his potential…" "If only she could play matches like she plays in practice…" "If only he wouldn't get tight during crucial points…" "If only she would just let herself go and play…" "He is so much better than this, but…" and so on and so forth? We all know the mental side of tennis is huge. Boris Becker once said, "Tiebreakers are 98% mental." Additionally, Dr. Alan Goldberg, noted sports psychology consultant, says, "In sports, the mental game is like the glue—it's what holds everything together."

The game is made up of four parts: technical, strategic, physical, and mental. One of these parts without the others is essentially worthless. You can think of it like a car. The technical part is the body—a stable foundation, streamlined to make the car travel smoothly. The strategic part is the steering wheel—able to travel in the desired direction, or change course whenever necessary. The physical part is the gas—physical preparation and stamina, the component ensuring that the car has the juice to complete the journey. The mental part is the engine—the most essential component, the force that starts the car and makes it run. When all of the above are working smoothly together, our tennis game runs like a brand new sports car, with high performance and no worries. Yet when one of the components goes awry, the whole machine malfunctions.

Knowing all this, the key question becomes: What gets in the way of a player performing well in pressure situations? More often than not, it is a result of fears which block the path towards potential unlimited performance. Oftentimes the player is aware of these fears but does not accept them, creating an internal struggle. Other times the fears may be just below their conscious thought patterns, and in this case it becomes necessary to delve a bit deeper into what is actually behind the fears. Following are seven of the biggest fears that can hold an athlete back from achieving their potential unlimited performance.

1. Fear of Not Being Good Enough: This fear rears its head all the time, both on and off the court; in fact just thinking about it may trigger an "a-ha" moment. We all want to believe in ourselves and feel that we have the ability to be successful, and anything short of that can be disheartening. In match play, players sometimes get discouraged and begin to fear that they are not good enough to compete with an opponent; they then lose their will and compete less than 100%. Sometimes in life, and tennis, setbacks may seem like a validation of not being good enough—that we lacked what it took to achieve. However, while we may have setbacks, what really determines our strength is how we respond to them.

2. Fear of Failure: This fear usually rears its head during a close match, especially when a player is perceived as being better than their opponent. The seemingly lesser player plays without expectations, but the favored player seems to be playing with a weight around their neck. The favored player is afraid to fail because they tie their identity and self-worth into their performance. Additionally, they may be afraid of what others think if they perform below expectations. Oftentimes when a player is afraid to experiment, afraid to try new techniques, or afraid to take a risk, their fear of failure is the cause.

3. Fear of the Unknown: This fear often rears its head in preparation for a big match. The player can't possibly know for sure whether they will win or lose. This "fear of the unknown" creates a high level of anxiety about what's going to happen, and then if "that happens" what "will happen" after that. Along with this is the fear of not being in control. This can be seen when a player is on the defensive. This player may over-hit, perhaps attempting a low-percentage winner, because they are so uncomfortable with their opponent dictating the point. However, being aware of their defensive positioning and accepting the situation will allow them to play solid defense, eventually working their way back to a neutral position.

4. Fear of Being Judged: This often comes up when a player is thinking about what their parents, coach, or teammates are thinking as they are playing. This simple act of curiosity takes the player away from their present situation on the court, towards something off the court that they can't control. It is here that unconditional acceptance from the support team is so important. When such support is provided, the player can feel calm, relaxed and safe. Thus, the player can play free without any worry of the results.

5. Fear of Not Meeting Expectations: This is similar to the fear of being judged, in that the player cannot control what someone else expects. Often the expectations of parents, coaches, and friends are solely focused on wins and losses. The process (the journey) is ignored. For a player to play their best, they must be in the present and focus on the experience. Focusing on expectations of winning creates a mental distraction.

6. Fear of Success: This fear manifests itself when a player has a lead and then begins to think things like, "I shouldn't be beating this person—they are ranked higher than me." Or, this player may not view him- or herself at a certain skill level, and therefore feel undeserving of a victory. Other times, the uncertainty and subsequent anxiety of putting themselves on the line for a possible victory is too much to handle. The certainty of losing, while disappointing, is well-known and a familiar road already traveled.

7. Fear of Injury or Re-Injury: This fear is referred to as the "silent epidemic" by sport psychologist Dr. David Grand. It is often driven by our macho sports culture's unwillingness to deal with the emotional stress and traumatic experiences that may result from injuries. Specifically neglected is the athlete's uncertainty about recovery, alienation from the team, fear of not being able to return at full strength, and even anxiety about what might happen should the situation recur. It's important to note that while the athlete may be cleared physically by doctors, emotionally they still may not have processed through the fear. Anyone who has experienced an injury understands how the mental scars don't just disappear when the doctor says you're cleared to play.

In today's sporting society, exhibiting any sign of weakness or fear is difficult for a player. Society views vulnerability as weakness, whereas in reality, awareness of vulnerability equates to true strength. Fears like the seven mentioned above crop up all the time, especially in pressure situations. They are a defense mechanism to prevent us from trying something which may make us uncomfortable. Yet, recognizing such fears and having the courage and support system to work through them is what truly enables us to grow and reach our individual potential.

" I'm playin' in the rain,
            Just playin' in the rain..."

Flight, Fight, Freeze

WORKOUT

The Seven Biggest Fears That Paralyze Athletes

Rate these fears in order of how they affect you:

_____ Fear of not being good enough   _____ Fear of not meeting expectations

_____ Fear of failure   _____ Fear of success

_____ Fear of the unknown   _____ Fear of injury/re-injury

_____ Fear of being judged   _____ other (did I miss one?)

Choose the top fear and write it down.

_____

When you think of this fear, what do you experience?

_____

_____

What is the scariest aspect about that fear?

_____

On a scale of 1 to 10 (10 being the most), how strong is the fear?_____

How do you experience the fear on the court (i.e. tight/restricting)?

_____

Where do you feel the fear in your body?

_____

Now, bring your attention to a time on the court when you felt calm. How did you experience it?

_____

Where do you feel the calm in your body?

_____

Now, take a minute to notice the calm.

Go back to noticing the fear... how do you experience it now?

_____

_____

Usually the fear will subside.

Workout 32
Mental Point

We often forget that behind the superstar athlete's exterior, the athlete is a person first and performer second.

I Can't Believe I Choked!
Understanding Slumps, Blocks and the Yips

What the Pros Are Saying

I'm obviously disappointed that I lost, but if I dwell on this, the next 25 tournaments I'm going to play this year probably would suck, too… I'm going to try to keep my head up and work as hard as I can.

> — **Sloane Stephens**, *Bleacher Report: What's Next for Sloane Stephens After Early 2015 Australian Open Exit?* by Carol Schram, 1/21/15

The things off court were not working for me. It reflected on my game, on my professional tennis career. It's been a big mental struggle because I was trying to separate my professional life from my more private life… If something isn't working off court, then it's going to reflect on the court. I managed to solve those problems.

> — **Novak Djokovic**, *Reuters: I went through big mental struggle* by Ian Ransom, 1/30/11

The unconscious accumulation of physical and emotional traumas in the athlete's brain and body are the root causes of all significant performance problems.

> — **Drs. Grand and Goldberg**, *This Is Your Brain on Sports*

Key Principles
1. When an athlete walks onto the court, their experiences, fears and traumas follow them.
2. Trust yourself, trust your game.

I Can't Believe I Choked!

How many times have you seen an athlete get tight, underperform, or choke in a big event? In practice they play great—not a care in the world, going for broke on every shot, and effortlessly succeeding while doing so. Yet once the competition starts, their best shots become their worst. Perhaps their big forehand, previously a weapon, turns defensive. Or maybe the formerly simple act of a two-foot putt now becomes unmanageable. Suddenly the reliable catcher can't make a routine throw back to the pitcher. Inexplicably, the runner hesitates during a pivotal point in the race. Fans become dumbfounded, and cannot believe that an elite athlete can succumb to this type of pressure. "How can this happen? What's the cause of this?" they ask.

In looking for the solution, many coaches, fans, players, media, and even performance experts start by critiquing what they can see (i.e. the double faults, missed free throws, or errant putts). Their initial intent is to look above the surface to find what's broken in hopes of a technical "quick fix." Certainly, this is the place to look if the situation occurs once or twice. However, if the choke or slump continues repeatedly under pressure, it falls in the category of a repetitive sports performance block.

A repetitive sports performance block (i.e. choke, slump, yips) is actually the *symptom* of an underlying issue. The *cause* is an accumulation of negative experiences from which the athlete has not been able to

move on. In actuality, this block has little to do with the last time the player "choked." Rather, something about that pressure situation was the trigger that brought the unprocessed issue to the surface where it distracted the athlete's performance. In fact, before or during the competition, some athletes are aware that "something is just not right." They experience underlying nervousness and anxiety and try to hide or resist it. Oftentimes, the athlete doesn't want to address their anxiety for fear of being judged by teammates or fans as lacking mental toughness. Yet other times, the athlete may be completely unaware of the root cause of their anxiety, since it has been disassociated from their consciousness in an effort to protect their personal psyche. Either way, the athlete's performance bears the burden.

Much like "heavy baggage" we hold onto on a daily basis, these negative experiences can grip a person and accumulate during a person's life from both on- and off-field incidents. Emotional trauma can come from situations such as embarrassment from double faulting in a big match, striking out with the bases loaded in the bottom of the ninth inning, or repeatedly missing putts on your short game. Physical trauma can derive from getting beaned with a ball, getting blindsided on the football field, or lying face down in pain after your ankle gave way on a wide forehand. Additionally, off-field trauma can occur and accumulate stemming from issues such as divorce, death, car accidents, or other circumstances. Similarly, excessive judgment, expectations, and opponent comparisons from parents, coaches, media, or friends can also unknowingly add weight to the burden of pressure and distract a player from playing freely.

Throughout our lives we encounter physical and emotional trauma. Depending upon the severity of these instances and our preparedness to meet them at the time, we sometimes successfully absorb and process through these encounters, and other times we do not. When we are unable to process these experiences, the stress does not evaporate over time. Rather, we store the unprocessed memory in the brain, where it may show itself at unexpected times. During a game, for instance, a baseball player who had been beaned by a pitch may be scared to get back in the batter's box, sometimes without admitting it to himself, and certainly not to his teammates. Or perhaps a tennis player may be so scared of losing or making the same error from previous matches that they tense up, hesitate, or even freeze during the match.

These unprocessed negative experiences can accumulate like balls in a bucket. Each individual issue represents a different size ball. Some may be small like the size of a golf ball, others bigger like a tennis ball, and others still bigger like a football, depending upon the level of stress and anxiety the person/athlete carries. These emotional/physical trauma-like experiences get held in the body's central nervous system. They directly interfere with the athlete's ability to access and adapt to situations and perform movements that were once so easy and instinctual. Finally, when a ball tumbles out of the bucket, the player's repetitive sports performance block is now on public display for all to see, judge, and evaluate.

We often forget that behind the superstar athlete's exterior, the athlete is a person first and a performer second. It's almost impossible not to be affected by the troubling day-to-day events which we all experience. Each person holds on to different things in different ways. James Blake summed it up best in his autobiography, Breaking Back, explaining, *"If there is something wrong in your life, it'll show up in your tennis game—not always in predictable ways... self-belief might be manifested in weak second serves, impatience can cause you to make low-percentage gambles, and so on."*

In summary, it's clear that we hold emotional (fears) and physical (injuries) trauma-like experiences in our bodies. As a person this "baggage" can consciously or unconsciously affect how we react, adapt, and adjust to everyday situations. As a player it can also carry onto the playing field and affect an athlete's ability to perform, especially in a high-pressure situation. In light of this, it makes sense to look beyond the slump, choke, or yips, below the surface to the root cause. The athlete is not broken, or a "head case," as some might suggest. The block is part of their process and actually can be a valuable clue to turning their situation around. Ultimately, they will emerge mentally stronger, move without hesitation, and compete with increased confidence.

I Can't Believe I Choked!

WORKOUT

Think of a time you choked or got really uptight... when was it? Where was it? Who were you playing?

_____

_____

_____

_____

What did you try to do at the time to try and manage the situation?

_____

_____

_____

_____

Describe in detail what happened, and what you experienced...

Before:_____

_____

_____

During:_____

_____

_____

After:_____

_____

_____

Has it happened in another area of your life, on or off the court? Describe it.

_____

_____

_____

_____

_____

_____

_____

Recognizing the above, what does this make you aware of?

_____

_____

_____

_____

_____

_____

_____

What are three things you could try next time as you feel yourself starting to get tense?

1. _____

2. _____

3. _____

Conclusion

What's Next?

Tennis Inside the Zone is intended to stimulate ideas, thoughts, and questions. Ultimately the workbook is intended to provide a foundation to help you become more self-aware, curious, and to embrace competition over the course of your athletic journey. Like any journey, different events and experiences will bring different insights—be aware of these insights and continually build on them.

Tennis Inside the Zone is meant to continually evolve and bring you back to a centered place, no matter where you are on your competitive journey. Because of this, I encourage you to revisit and reassess the workouts throughout your journey. In my experience, any path to improvement is one step at a time. This process must be encountered with patience, purpose, and perseverance, both for others and for yourself. This reminds me of the Chinese proverb, "a journey of a thousand miles starts with a single step."

Now that you have read and experienced **Tennis Inside the Zone**, I thank you for your time and hope you have found it both rewarding and thought-provoking. Please share with me your insights, experiences, successes, failures, obstacles, and tipping points. I genuinely look forward to reconnecting in my future books, workshops, or consultations.

My Next Step...

As I mentioned, like your personal journey, mine is also evolving. In the Introduction I mentioned how this book started with my clients asking me questions related to mental training. Little did I know at the time that it would eventually lead to me publishing my first book!

But as we know, no journey is complete without the next step... My next step is to choose certain key chapters and expand on them in another book. With this in mind, I have already begun writing a book called *Winning from the Inside Out: The Athlete is a Person First and a Performer Second.* Additionally, I am working on a book called *Competeology: What Does it Take to Win?* And of course, *Parenting Inside the Zone* and *Coaching Inside the Zone.*

B'simcha (with happiness)

Rob

P.S. If you want to chat more, share an idea, experience, or thought, agree or disagree with something I said, please contact me at:

- rob@insidethezone.com

- www.insidethezone.com

- 973-723-0314

I'll look forward to hearing from you!

Praise for *Inside The Zone...*

What the players are saying...

"Working with Rob has been a great experience. He has helped me out with my tennis game dramatically, from determination to sportsmanship. His strategies and techniques for teaching the mental side of tennis, along with all other sports, are beneficial to anyone he works with. I had a one-hour session with Rob this morning and felt like a new person on the court. Truly amazing stuff."

— Jack, Tennis

"Rob and I worked together at the Bangalore Tennis Center. Before he came I was serving well, however I had been working to get a bit extra on my serve. It was almost like magic: he asked me to notice the lift feeling I was getting in my legs on my old serve. I soon realized that my legs were not generating the power they were capable of. He then asked me to serve with my eyes closed, explode off the ground, and notice the feeling in my legs. It was almost as if I was flying! Rob then advised me to be aware of where I felt this new serve in my body. Immediately I felt it in my thighs, the explosion was so powerful. With this newfound awareness, I integrated the big lift and immediately picked up at least another 10-15 mph on my serve. Now when I step to the line, I just remember the feeling and go out and hit big serves. I am truly grateful for the work we did together."

— Aditya, Tennis

"Working with Rob has made me more confident. It has allowed me to enjoy playing tennis more than I ever have in my life. Accepting where I am as a tennis player has paved the way for me to play free. Not only have I gone through this change as a tennis player, but I have changed as a person too. What Rob taught me is applicable to so many other situations in life. He helped me understand that what I learned in the realm of tennis— accepting myself as a player, accepting my nervousness during a match, enjoying the game—can be used outside the court. I am very thankful that I am working with Rob because he has made me a better tennis player and a better person."

— Andy, Tennis

"Life is just sweeter with the inner joy that tennis brings. It's not necessarily the Ws, but more the isolated incidences on court where magic happens... that feeling of euphoria as brilliance leaves your strings, and you know for that moment, you're a star... shining bright. I am in constant chase of those moments, like an addict in search of the next high. And what I have learned from you, Rob, is that I was searching too hard. The craving of that rush was so strong that I forced everything, instead of just letting it happen. And now when the magic happens, it's authentic, which solidifies that the talent has always been there. I just had to get out of my own way."

— Kellie, Adult Tennis

"Working with Rob has helped me trust myself, play within myself, manage my nerves, reduce my expectations, and focus on the process of real competition. Since I began working with Rob, I now am able to relax on court because I have accepted who I am as a tennis player. Rob is always there for me whether it is to encourage, motivate, pump up, relax, talk, or simply listen before big matches... he usually has the ideal quote to put you inside the ZONE."

— **Dean, Tennis**

What the parents are saying...

"Rob is the consummate professional. I have seen first hand his desire, knowledge and work ethic. Moreover, the most important factor is the fact that Rob's work definitely creates results. I have seen a measurable improvement regarding the work he has done with my daughter."

— **Bob, Tennis Dad**

"Since working with Rob my daughter's competitive results have changed in a positive way. She accepts that she is control of the things that she can control, and is better at embracing those that she cannot. Her match play is more relaxed and for the most part she enjoys competing. Most important, she realizes that while results are important, her focus needs to be on the process by staying in the moment. From there, the results she desires will come."

— **Allen, Tennis Dad**

"Thank you for working with my daughter. She really appreciated your energy! She said she became much more aware of what she was trying to do with the ball now. You are integral to the athlete! Thank you again for all the help!"

— **Laura, Tennis Mom**

"Our son is a junior tennis player and he has been working with Rob on various aspects of his mental game. Since that time we have seen a tremendous improvement in his game. We have also seen a noticeable change in his attitude off the court too. Our son enjoys his sessions with Rob and feels very comfortable with Rob. He feels Rob is trustworthy and understanding. As parents, we are particularly appreciative for Rob's efforts to continuously keep us in the loop. Rob gives us constructive suggestions on how to best help our son with his mental game on and off the court."

— **Stephen, Tennis Dad**

"Working with Rob has raised my daughter's game to the next level. Rob is a patient listener and has the best intentions in helping his clients. Rob's positive outlook and tips have made the experience worthwhile."

— **Mike, Tennis Dad**

"I already feel incredibly evolved and enlightened thanks to our great discussion and your terrific follow up articles, all of which I have read and will re-read. It is incredible how precisely these articles describe the reality. What a gift that we found you—I can't thank you enough. My personal mantra moving forward—trust, empower, detach, have fun, enjoy... chill!! Let's see if I can live up to the challenge!"

— **Cindy, Tennis Mom**

"As most tennis parents we have invested a lot of time and effort towards our kid's junior tennis career... working with Rob has been without a doubt the most rewarding experience of all. Within a few weeks we have been able to see a substantial change in our daughter's mental attitude, not only in the tennis court but outside of it as well. Also as an added benefit, it has helped me to understand the pressures she goes through as a player and therefore to develop a better relationship with her. In retrospect I wish we had crossed paths with Rob a few years ago. This has been an awesome journey. THANK YOU Rob for everything you have done for us!"

— Carlos, Tennis Dad

"Rob's workshop for parents was very insightful. As a parent, it felt very comforting to know that ALL the other parents in the room had the same issues and experiences with their children that we have with ours. Discovering that other families also experience horrible rides home from tournaments was eye-opening! Rob is extremely empathetic and was familiar with every issue the parents discussed in the workshop. He had calm, logical perspective on situations that come up, but did not mask the fact that all issues take work, they do not solve themselves overnight. Our son has achieved much success working with Rob."

— Sue, Tennis Mom

What the coaches are saying...

"We have seen firsthand how Rob's work has positively impacted players, both as a person and a tennis player. His program is a must for anyone who wants to break through to the next level."

— Tim Mayotte, former #7 professional in the world. Mayotte, Hurst, Stevenson Tennis Academy

"Rob's ideas are inspiring and motivating for kids and coaches. His talk to New Jersey high school coaches on Coaching the Mental Game was informative and interesting. While his talk was sport-specific, much of it applies to improving in life skills."

— Elliot Lovi, Livingston High School Tennis Coach

"Rob is one of our nation's top mental training coaches today! His seminar at the annual ITA Coaches' Convention was entertaining, educational, and spot-on regarding the challenges college coaches face. Tennis parents, players, and coaches could and should use a large dosage of Rob's ideas and perspective to navigate through the rough and tumble world of competitive tennis and all sports."

— Ed Krass, Founder/ Director College Tennis Exposure Camp & One-On-One Doubles Tennis Events

"Rob's workshop entitled 'Break Point or Break Down—Concentrate to Win,' at the Ramat HaSharon Israeli Tennis Center (ITC) for our staff of 30 sport psychologists and head tennis coach was both dynamic and interesting. His energy level and his passion came across to all of us who participated. Most importantly he left us with tools that we can use when we work with our athletes on a day-to-day basis. We are looking forward to hosting him again."

— Dr. Ellen Katz, Director, Center for Sport Psychology, Israel Tennis Center, Ramat HaSharon, Israel

"It was a pleasure hosting Rob at the High Performance Tennis Center (HPTC) being run at the Karnataka State Lawn Tennis Association (KSLTA) tennis complex in India. I appreciate his commitment towards the sport. His interaction and the approach towards the mental side of the game was indeed a big eye-opener for all of us. Rob's approach to the psychological side of tennis is extremely creative and informative. His enthusiasm and sincerity is evident.

"Afterwards Rob worked privately on the court with two top-500 players in the world. He helped one of them find a natural rhythm to his ground strokes. The student referred to it as 'freeing his hands.' The other student he worked with on 'feeling the explosion' from his legs during the service motion. As a result the student began serving in the 118 miles-per-hour range. We look forward to Rob returning to India for a longer period of time and continuing to work with our kids in Bangalore and Delhi. He would be an asset to our program."

— Sunil Yajaman, WTA Bangalore Open, Director — HPTC KSLTA Tennis Stadium, Cubbon Park, Bangalore 560001 INDIA

"Coaches, forget about ordering a therapist couch to replace the sideline bench! Bring Polishook's new book *Tennis Inside the Zone* to practice sessions, rainy day chalk talks and matches. You'll soon be able to relax while your players stop making excuses, play the key points with ease, and learn how to compete in big match situations."

— Ira Miller, Tennis Coach NJIT. Mens and Womens

"Rob can relate to on & off-court issues that tennis tennis players experience. His work is not just with athletes in a slump or with fears, but also helping high-achieving athletes break beyond barriers."

— Jeff Rothstein, USPTA Tennis Pro

Biography of the Author

Rob Polishook, M.A., C.P.C., is founder and director of Inside the Zone Sports Performance Group, LLC. As a mental training coach, he works with athletes and teams from junior players to professionals, helping them to uncover their mental edge—often the difference between winning and losing. He specializes in helping athletes overcome performance blocks (i.e. yips, chokes, slumps, anxiety), helping athletes work through the "unspoken" psychological trauma from injuries, helping already high-performing athletes reach beyond self-imposed barriers, and teaching innovative mental training skills, tools, and techniques.

Rob's non-judgmental manner encourages athletes to work with performance issues using awareness, acceptance, and brain/body intuition. This unique inside-out approach encourages empowerment and trust in self and the process. Rob's focus is on the athlete as a person first and a performer second. Through this lens, he recognizes that day-to-day on- and off-the-court/field experiences directly impact how an athlete performs, especially under pressure.

Internationally, Rob has presented workshops in India at the Karnataka Lawn and Tennis Association in Bangalore for high performance juniors. Additionally, he presented his USTA-Eastern District award-winning presentation, entitled "Breakthrough on Break Points—Concentrate to Win," at Ramat HaSharon,

the flagship location of the Israeli Tennis Center, to their sport psychology staff, coaches and juniors. Nationally, Rob has presented workshops for colleges and high school teams in all sports. He has presented for the USPTA, USTA, ITA, and NJSIAA. He regularly runs week-long workshops called "Unleashing the Performer Within" at the highly acclaimed Omega Institute.

Rob's articles have been published nationally and internationally and he has been quoted in *Sports Illustrated*. He has also been featured in interviews with ESPN radio and TennisChannel.com.

Rob is an accomplished athlete and USPTA certified coach. As a high school coach, he received the 2007 Coach of the Year Award for high school women's tennis in Union County, NJ. He also received the 2008 USPTA Eastern Division's High School Coach of the Year Award. Additionally, he has coached the 16-and-under USTA-Eastern Zonal team.

Rob has earned a Masters degree in psychological studies with a concentration in sport and exercise psychology from Seton Hall University (SHU), and has completed his certification in sport psychology from SHU. He is a certified professional/life coach from IPEC, an international federation coaching affiliate. He has also received certifications in Somatic Experiencing, Brainspotting Sports Performance Work, Focusing and Jim Loehr's Mental Toughness Program.

Rob and his wife Debbie live in New York City. He can often be spotted playing on the red clay Riverside tennis courts, har-tru Central Park courts, or running with Debbie in Central Park.

Gumbo, Deb, and I at the Indian Wells Tournament
(Deb took the picture!)

About Inside the Zone Sports Performance Group

Founded in 2005, Inside the Zone Sports Performance Group was born from Rob Polishook's passion for sports, his love of working with kids, and his curiosity in understanding the process of what it takes to help athletes break beyond barriers. The goal of Inside the Zone Sports Performance Group is to assist athletes, in all sports and at all levels, to uncover their mental edge and unleash their unlimited peak performance.

The mental side plays a large role in any sport. In fact, with all the club teams and increased specialization among teams, it is interesting, and even remiss, that the real mental issues regarding competition among young athletes are not being addressed. These issues include, but are not limited to, competing under pressure; handling setbacks and using them to bounce back; concentrating under pressure; staying centered; focusing on the process and not on the scoreboard; crafting strategies for goal setting; and reaching beyond self-imposed barriers toward limitless peak potential. Inside the Zone Sports Performance Group's mission is to address these issues and more.

Inside the Zone Sports Performance Group services:

- One-on-one and group consultations for athletes, parents, and coaches

- Workshops and seminars for teams, parents, and coaches

- Dynamic season-long consultations for teams

Rob Polishook, M.A., C.P.C.
Mental Training Coach
www.insidethezone.com
rob@insidethezone.com

Play!

Play Proud

Play with Heart

Play like a Champion

Play **insidethezone.com**

About Rob: The Back Story

Who am I?

I was born imperfect—or maybe perfectly imperfect! Here's a great example from my first grade class trip: All I remember is spinning around a revolving door at the Empire State Building, getting my shoe caught and holding up everyone from access to the door for three minutes, while being laughed at by my class. Then, back in the classroom, I was unable to read: the letters were a jumbled mess, teachers would get frustrated, and I was ashamed to raise my hand. I was diagnosed with a form of dyslexia and a motor learning problem.

I vividly remember being left behind in first grade, and attempting to explain the reason to my friends. Even clearer was my memory of getting special tutoring from Mrs. Schaffer after school on reading, writing and arithmetic. Going into third grade I couldn't read or write cursive, and this presented a problem. It felt like I was in a foreign country. The only place I might have felt normal was Hebrew school, but here I didn't understand the letters either! In my spare time, I remember balancing on a board, the kind with a roller underneath, which was supposed to help with my coordination and balance.

I did these types of exercises my entire childhood! Extra work was something that was part of my upbringing. I never had time to feel sorry for myself or ask why I was different; I just went to the extra tutoring and got on my balance board for hours.

I learned at an early age never, never, never to give up. I never let an opportunity for extra credit pass by. And I never stopped training at anything I cared about.

I was lucky. At an early age I experienced what it was like to have a strong support system, with parents who believed in me. Because of my learning disabilities, I learned to be empathetic to others who didn't get things done as fast or as well as the rest of the class.

Why am I writing this book?

Every day, I hear athletes tell me about their fears, anxieties, and performance blocks. I hear how they are serving for a match and they can't grip their racket; or how they stand on a pitcher's mound feeling like they are on a deserted island; or how they constantly get caught in a negative spiral during pressure situations. It reminds me of how when I was a kid, I wished I had someone I could open up to and let them know how I was feeling and experience a situation from my point of view. Instead, my coaches always told me how I was supposed to be feeling and what I could or couldn't do. If nothing else, a book like this would have been valuable just to have an outlet to let go, and in some cases verify what I was thinking was "normal."

After I listen to what my clients are saying, I usually express to them that they are not alone in what they are thinking and feeling; in fact, it's often shared by many athletes in the same situation on all levels. This reassurance usually makes them feel like a 500-pound weight has been lifted off their shoulders. Then, when I tell them that they are not broken and don't need fixing, that rather the answers lie within, and that we just need to uncover them, they usually take a big sigh, and exhale in relief.

Acknowledgements

Metaphorically, I view life as a patchwork quilt. Each patch represents a person who has had an impact on me. No matter where the patch's (person's) location on the quilt, each is special and unique in its own way. Please know that if you are a family member, friend, colleague or acquaintance, you are an important part of my life experience. Thank you!

My first mentor in the world of sport psychology was Dr. Jena Marcovicci. His gentle, playful, and gracious spirit lives with me each day. Dr. Alan Goldberg and Dr. David Grand have been great mentors and friends. Both have been instrumental in guiding and teaching me, espe-cially the foundational idea that an athlete is a person first and a performer second, and al-ways to take the time to understand how the athlete/person is experiencing things through their eyes. I have spent countless hours with them over the years and am so grateful for their continued support and encouragement. Thanks to Mackey Sasser for allowing Dr. Grand, Dr. Goldberg, and myself to work with you and being a friend.

Thanks to Lee Hurst, with whom I have spent countless hours sharing ideas and chatting about tennis; our conversations continue to be full of learning. Thanks to Phil Stevenson, Carl Thorsen, Tim Mayotte, Jeff Brandes, Ed Krass, Elliot Lovi, Carol Smith, Clay Bibbee, and Ira Miller with whom I also share ideas and who have been very supportive of my work. Thanks to Julie Bliss, Jeff Rothstein, Danny Casesa, and Esu Maat, my partners from USTA Zonals. Thanks to Mike Sandor, Brian Erikson, Peter Tierney, and Rob Grella of Summit High School, and William Martin of Oratory Prep where I got my start coaching and developing workshops for your athletic teams. Special thanks to John Martini, Justin Ferrante, and Peter Seneca, who are always available to share ideas, trends, and critique my work. Lastly, Nancy Ho whose memory and vision will never be forgotten.

Thanks to Ava and Steve Schlesinger, Skye Marcovicci, Dr. Chris Rank, Dr. Sandra Lee, Dr. Ste-phen Walker, Dr. Michael Sachs, Dr. Ellen Katz, Dr. Riley Nickols, Dr. Jerry Lynch, Dr. Rob Gilbert, Greg Chertok, Gina Karnisova, Janice Campbell, Howard Smith, Jeff Shalan, Forsan Hussein, Michael Wagner, Rob Wagner, Kathleen Horvath, Ron Becker, Sunil Yajamin, Anjan Viplav, Bob Litwin, Rob Delaney, and Roger Flax.

Thanks to Kellie Patterson for her creative cover designs, great ideas, and keen eye regarding all graphic and design standards throughout each page of the book. Justin Cooke, David Sison, and Idalia Williford for your help with my articles. John Solie, a.k.a. "Penner," for his patience to advance this book into final production. Ethan Saal the quote man.

Thanks to Martin Rouillard for believing in this book and my ideas. And to Ian Halperin for believing in me, my ideas and work! Also for introducing me to Martin. To Suzanne Kingsbury who always encourages and has kind words to share.

I am so grateful to each and every one of my clients. You know who you are! Through you I have learned; you have opened up to me with your deepest fears and aspirations. You have allowed me to help you achieve your greatest successes. Thank you to all the parents who have trusted me while I do my work.

Thanks to my Dad, Shimmy, and my Mum, Jean: her devotion to inspire others lives inside of me. My brother Mark, sister Janis, sister/brother-in-laws Janet, Robin, Kevin, Mark, Sandy, in-laws Sandy, Lenny, and our precious nieces and nephews.

Lastly, but most importantly, my bride of 27 years, Debbie. None of this work could ever have been begun without your unconditional love, support, and belief in me. You listen to all my crazy ideas and encourage me to pursue most of them! You have been my rock.

One step at a time...

and while your stepping, breathe!

Sources

I would like to take a moment to acknowledge some of the books where I have gathered many quotes, stories, or have been fortunate enough to learn from many of the authors who have come before me. Their works/teachings have had a great impact on my ideas and continue to serve as a foundation and guiding light. Thank you!

- Agassi, Andre. *Open*. New York: AKA Publishing, 2009.

- Blake, James with Andrew Friedman. *Breaking Back*. New York: HarperCollins, 2007.

- Dweck, Carol S., PhD. *Mindset*. New York: Random House, 2006.

- Freeman, Criswell. *The Tennis Lover's Book of Wisdom*. Nashville: Walnut Grove Press, 1997.

- Gallwey, Timothy W. *The Inner Game of Tennis*. New York: Random House, 1997.

- Goldberg, Alan, Ph.D., *Sports Slump Busting*. Florida: Llumina Press, 2005.

- Grand, David, Ph.D., and Alan Goldberg, Ph.D. *This is Your Brain on Sports*. Indianapolis: Dog Ear Publishing, 2011.

- Grand, David, Ph.D. *Brainspotting: A Revolutionary New Therapy for Rapid and Effective Change*. Louisville: Sounds True 2013

- Jackson, Susan A., Ph.D., and Mihaly Csikszentmihalyi, Ph.D. *Flow in Sports*. United States: Human Kinetics, 1999.

- King, Billie Jean. *Pressure is a Privilege*. New York: Life Time Media, 2008.

- Levine, Peter A. Ph.D. *Waking the Tiger*. California: North Atlantic Books, 1997.

- Lynch, Jerry, Ph.D., and Chungliang Al Huang, *The Way of the Champion*. Vermont: Tuttle Publishing, 2006.

- Marcovicci, Jena, Ph.D. *The Dance of Tennis*. Massachusetts, 1997.

- Perlstein, Scott. *The Quotable Tennis Player*. Connecticut: The Lyons Press, 2002.

Made in the USA
Middletown, DE
09 September 2019